W9-BLK-877

Rediscovering the Sunday School

Talmadge Johnson
Stan Toler

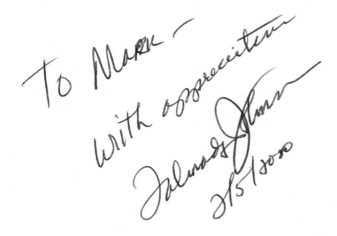

Beacon Hill Press of Kansas City
Kansas City, Missouri

10   9   8   7   6   5   4   3   2   1

To my parents, W. T. and Helen Johnson, both of whom have achieved the objective of their lives—a home in heaven. In their journey they left a legacy of commitment to Christ and the church that was especially demonstrated in their influential leadership through the Sunday School. In his years as a pastor and district superintendent, my father put Sunday School on the front burner of importance. Mother was a faithful and effective Sunday School teacher that believed in, and practiced, the principles of outreach, caring, and teaching. Many persons were won to Christ because of their devotion to a "people-focused and purpose-driven" Sunday School.

W. Talmadge Johnson

To my favorite teachers: Edith Shook, Evelyn McFarland, JoAn Allison, Esther Molin, David Case, and Dr. Elmer Towns.

Stan Toler

Contents

Special Thanks

To:
Deloris Leonard, Terry Toler, Jeffrey Johnson, Jeanne Griffin, and Pat Diamond.

Hardy Weathers, Kelly Gallagher, Bonnie Perry, Bruce Nuffer, Mike Estep, and the entire Beacon Hill team. Thanks for your investment in the project.

The Sunday School Ministries and WordAction teams—Jeanne Hubbs, David Felter, Randy Cloud, Lynda Boardman, David Caudle, Blaine Smith, and Mark York.

Jerry Brecheisen for editorial guidance, creative direction, and friendship!

Stan Toler

About the Authors

Dr. Talmadge Johnson is the general director of Sunday School Ministries for the International Church of the Nazarene.

A graduate of Southern Nazarene University, Johnson received the bachelor of arts and the master of arts degrees in religion. Ordained in 1958 on the Southwest Oklahoma District, Johnson served as an evangelist from 1958 to 1961. He pastored Elk City, Oklahoma, from 1961 to 1965. From 1965 to 1975, he was the founding pastor of the Oklahoma City Western Oaks Church. Johnson served as superintendent of the Mississippi District from 1975 to 1980 and the Tennessee District from 1980 to 1994.

Johnson was general president of Nazarene Young People's Society from 1972 to 1976. He also served on the General Board from 1972 to 1976 and 1980 to 1994. He was chairman of the World Mission Department of the General Board from 1986 to 1994. He was honored with the doctor of divinity degree by Trevecca Nazarene University in 1983.

He and his wife, Genell, have two sons, Michael and Jeffrey, who with their families serve in special ministries in the Church of the Nazarene.

To contact the author:
Dr. W. Talmadge Johnson
International Church of the Nazarene
6401 The Paseo
Kansas City, MO 64131

Dr. Stan Toler is a gifted leader, administrator, and inspirational speaker. He is known as a "pastor to pastors."

In addition to training church leaders throughout North America, he serves as the senior pastor of Trinity Church of the Nazarene in Oklahoma City, Oklahoma, and hosts the television program *Leadership Today.*

As model church instructor for INJOY Group, a leadership development institute for pastors, Stan conducts seminars on strategic planning, stewardship, outreach, and leadership throughout the United States.

Author of over 30 books and manuals on the subjects of church ministry, evangelism, and "helps" for pastors, Stan communicates with witty enthusiasm and practical insight his zeal for touching lives through the ministry of the church.

He and his wife, Linda, have two sons, Seth and Adam.

For additional information on seminars, scheduling speaking engagements, or to contact the author:

Stan Toler
P.O. Box 950
Bethany, OK 73008
E-mail: stoler1107@aol.com

Introduction

Folk-rock musician Dave Swarbrick made a startling discovery as he read the obituary column of a well-known British newspaper: he was listed in it. Though he was in the hospital for a chest infection, he certainly didn't qualify for inclusion in the obits. The embarrassed newspaper printed their retraction the next day.

Nehemiah could have been discouraged by the obituaries in the newspaper of his day. The walls of his beloved city were in ruins. His hopes and dreams seemed pulverized like the crushed stone of the walls. His detractors seemed to spell an eternal doom for the city and its ruined walls. But the story of reconstruction and renewal is very familiar. In the face of the ruins, Nehemiah had a burden for rebuilding. His actions are important: (1) He wept over them, (2) He asked God for a plan, (3) He organized for effectiveness, (4) He recruited helpers, and (5) He went to work. The rest is truly history:

So we rebuilt the wall till all of it reached half its height, for the people worked with all their heart. But when Sanballat, Tobiah, the Arabs, the Ammonites and the men of Ashdod heard that the repairs to Jerusalem's walls had gone ahead and that the gaps were being closed, they were very angry. . . .

Meanwhile, the people in Judah said, "The strength of the laborers is giving out, and there is so much rubble that we cannot rebuild the wall." . . .

Therefore I stationed some of the people behind the lowest points of the wall at the exposed places, posting them by families, with their swords, spears and bows. . . .

When our enemies heard that we were aware of their plot and that God had frustrated it, we all returned to the wall, each to his own work *(Neh. 4:6-15).*

Likewise, some have prematurely written their "obits" for the Sunday School movement. Though it has experienced its share of battles, and in some cases, the walls are cracked and crumbling, its demise is greatly exaggerated! On the other hand, in many churches Sunday School is seeing an ever-increasing resurgence.

Why? Like Nehemiah's troops, the people have a mind to work! Multiplied thousands of dedicated servants of the Lord are sacrificing time, treasure, and talent to rebuild the walls of Sunday School. And it's working! From creative small-group ministries to large church day schools, the battle for the souls of people is being waged valiantly.

One Burning Heart

In 1780, a man's heart burned with compassion for rowdy street children in England. Robert Raikes believed that preventing a problem was easier than trying to cure it. He turned to education. His approach was novel but effective. In the first Sunday School staff appointment, Raikes recruited a woman who opened her home to children from poor families. There, he offered the children a chance to learn and to be loved. And from that heartwarming effort an entire Sunday School movement emerged.

Conditions today are not unlike those of Raikes's time. Sadly, children lacking love and nurture roam our streets as well as the corridors of our schools and other public places. Rather than launching another movement to deal with the problem, we have a tremendous opportunity: to revitalize the powerful Sunday School movement.

A *Religion Today* Internet report of April 27, 1999, declared, "More than 2 billion people worldwide will be Christians in 2000." In the same report, researchers David Barrett and Todd Johnson estimate that "there are 1.99 billion people who profess Christianity today, about one-third of the world's population." The church possesses an awesome challenge: to minister with Spirit-empowered purpose and passion. The cry of a despairing world, searching for hope and answers, beckons today's church hearing the call of the Word. The world at its worst needs the church at its best.

Reignite the Fires of People-Driven Sunday Schools

This book is a challenge to reignite the fires of ministry passion for reaching the lost and discipling the found through Sunday Schools; Sunday Schools organized to fulfill a renewed purpose. Dr. Roy Zuck in his book *The Holy Spirit in Your Teaching* once defined that purpose as "the Christ-centered, Bible-based, pupil-related process of communicating God's written Word through the power of the Holy Spirit, for the purpose of leading pupils to Christ, and building them up in Christ."[1]

We must always remember, however, that *people are more important than processes.* Raikes had a vision for *people.* He was *people-driven.* He understood that the effectiveness of his ministry depended on being *people-focused.* It is a burden from the heart of the Good Shepherd who knows no rest until a solitary and needy sheep is safe in the fold.

We pray that Sunday School leaders and workers everywhere will recapture the joy of their mission: to reach people, teach people, and help people grow in God's grace. Religious research indicates it can be done. One study revealed that three out of five growing churches in North America have a strong adult Sunday School ministry, and that four out of five of those growing churches have strong children's Sunday School ministries.

A glorious new day is dawning for the Sunday School! New methods, new organizational structures, and new opportunities for training invite us. Your local church ministry can experience a renewal of this vision: Sunday School—great potential for outreach and for Christian education.

Our intent in this book is to give you a new glimpse into the exciting possibilities in Sunday School. You will learn to mix the traditional with the timely in methods of Bible study, organization, staffing, promotion, and facilities. In the next few pages you will discover how to:

- view Sunday School as a new paradigm
- stay focused on the Word
- evangelize through Sunday School ministries
- organize your Sunday School via multiple options
- use fellowship as a tool to reach new people
- promote the Sunday School with new methods
- use your current facilities for growth
- place a new emphasis on teaching basic Christian beliefs

Robert Raikes's burden and vision can be reborn in the hearts of believers who love the Savior, the One who sacrificed himself to reach people. This passion can be reborn in the hearts of willing workers who fall on their faces before God—the Father who waits to respond with His wisdom and power.

Rediscovering the Importance of Sunday School

*Only be careful, and watch yourselves closely so that you
do not forget the things your eyes have seen or let them
slip from your heart as long as you live. Teach them to
your children and to their children after them.*
(Deut. 4:9)

IN THE AFTERMATH of the tragic 1999 Columbine High School shooting rampage in Littleton, Colorado, a memorial was erected in the parking lot. The car of one shooting victim became the focal point for those who mourned the terrible loss. Before a tent was erected over the vehicle, and before the flowers were piled all around it, and before the messages of love and sympathy were taped to it, a news camera zoomed in to an object lying on the dashboard. There for all the world to see, was the study Bible of the car's owner. She, along with over 80 of her classmates, was part of a Bible study group in the school.

Before the tragic shot in the head, another classmate, Cassie, was asked if she believed in God. According to eyewitnesses, she hesitated for a moment, knowing what would happen if she answered in the affirmative. "Yes!" she strongly replied, in the last words that would ever fall from her lips. Earlier that brave young victim had made a videotape of her testimony following her conversion at a youth retreat. In it she expressed that living for Christ was the most important thing in life. It was so important to her that she was willing to die for it!

Someone taught those two young people in Sunday School. Someone led their Bible study group. Someone sacrificed time away from home, tedious hours of preparation, and careful intercession to make the retreat possible where a young martyr learned to love Jesus. Someone understood that teaching faith and values to the next generation was worth every effort!

Off to a Great Start

Sunday School may have lost its prominence at times, but it has never lost its importance. The transmission of God's truth is a vital part of church history. In fact, the church grew explosively after a Bible lesson in Jerusalem: "Then Peter stood up with the Eleven, raised his voice and addressed the crowd: 'Fellow Jews and all of you who live in Jerusalem, let me explain this to you; listen carefully to what I say'" (Acts 2:14).

The signs and wonders of that Pentecost day stirred the hearts of the tourists in town for the Jewish festival. Following the apostle Peter's sermon-lesson, over 3,000 people responded and were born to faith that day. They would need further instruction in the words and ways of the Lord.

Most of the converts were from the Jewish tradition. They naturally migrated to the Temple for worship and instruction. But soon they began to meet in small house-churches each week to celebrate the resurrection of Christ (see Acts 2:42-43). Those meetings became centers of instruction where God's Word was explored. And from those meetings, the disciples went into the marketplace to practice what they had learned.

Religious persecution sent many of the new converts packing. They became refugees driven from their beloved homeland into various parts of the world. And, wherever they ended up, a center of Christian instruction started up. "Now those who had been scattered by the persecution in connection with Stephen traveled as far as Phoenicia, Cyprus and Antioch, telling the message only to Jews. Some of them, however, men from Cyprus and Cyrene, went to Antioch and began to speak to Greeks also, telling them the good news about the Lord Jesus. The Lord's hand was with them, and a great number of people believed and turned to the Lord" (Acts 11:19-21).

History affirms that wherever Christians migrated, they met regularly for instruction, fellowship, and worship. Constantine's edict that nationalized Christianity pressed groups of scholars into spiritual service to exegete biblical truths. Colleges and universities sprang up and prepared students to minister to hearts hungry for the Word.

Then came the Wesleys. "Methodists" became their moniker because of their participation in the "methodical" small-group Bible studies at Oxford. John Wesley through the Methodists began instructing believers in "class meetings." These were meetings not only of instruction but also of fellowship, care, growth in the Christian disciplines, prayer, and evangelism. In an atmosphere of "tough love," believers were carefully questioned about their walk with the Lord and encouraged to practice their faith in daily living. The class leader asked each attendee for an account of how he or she lived the Christian life during the previous week. Accountability was one key to the spiritual growth of the class participants.

Wesley's influence set a spark burning in others who added the dimension of reaching the lost, as well as discipling the found, in small-group settings.

Sunday School's Marvelous Story

The first Sunday School began in Gloucester, England. Its purpose was not only to curb the rowdiness of street children but also to furnish an education to those children who were prevented from attending schools because of their employment. The Sunday School phenomenon spread quickly. By 1786, over 250,000 children were attending.

Our friend Dr. Elmer Towns, a tireless advocate of Sunday School, highlights the Sunday School's rich but oft forgotten legacy:

- The International Uniform Lesson began in 1866 with the vision of the whole world studying the same lesson each week.

- The *Sunday School Times* at one time was the world's largest magazine.

- A Sunday School parade took eight hours to pass the reviewing stand in Washington, D.C. (1904), and all but two members of Congress marched, carrying a Bible.

The influence of Sunday Schools continued. A Boston shoe salesman left his job to begin missions work in Chicago. From the Sunday School he started as part of his ministry, a church grew that is now known as Moody Memorial Church. In the turbulent '60s and into the '70s, a great convention of Sunday School enthusiasts held large rallies under the banner of the Mid America Sunday School Convention. It was headed by a true Sunday School champion, Clate Raymond. Thousands gathered for the workshops on teaching, bus ministry, child evangelism, and so forth. In 1976, a Sunday School teacher from Plains, Georgia, was elected to the presidency. Jimmy Carter became one of the most famous Sunday School teachers in history. In this same period, used buses were pressed into service and packed with enthusiastic children, who were often fed breakfast on their way to Sunday School. By the mid-'80s there were an estimated 29.7 million Sunday School students in the United States.

In the '90s, Sunday School graph lines began to go south. Toler and Towns, in their Leading the Sunday School conferences, point to several reasons for the decline:

- Lack of leadership
- Poor image
- Inadequate instruction
- Multiple worship services

- Wealth and riches
- Growth of privatized Christianity
- Declining regular attendance
- Small-group focus
- Time
- Change in methods

"Billy Sunday? Wow, he must have been good.
They named the day after him!"

Questions of Relevance

Does Sunday School work anymore? Responses to this question all depend on what the local church is doing with the Sunday School. If it is viewed as a mere perpetuation of a structured system, it is probably adrift and floundering for meaning and purpose. If, however, it is viewed by the pastor and lay leadership as *important,* the Sunday School is probably alive and well. It all depends on a *vision of the harvest* and the *priorities of the leaders.*

Dr. Russell Human, superintendent of Northeast Oklahoma District Church of the Nazarene, recently wrote a letter to his pastors. The priority for Sunday School is obvious as Human writes:

If any program-based methodology proved to be a dynamic tool for evangelistic churches, it was the Sunday School program. Most of the leaders of these churches were amused at the prophecies of the decline or death of Sunday School.

The problem with nonevangelistic Sunday Schools is not the program itself; the problem is the failure to use the program as an intentional evangelistic tool. Sunday School was the third-highest response when we asked these churches about the reasons for their evangelistic effectiveness.

Will the Sunday School survive? Yes! It has and it will. In fact, Thom Rainer states it very well in his book *Giant Awakenings:* "Sunday School will survive into the 21st century because it teaches the whole counsel of God across all generations. It has a great mission."[1] Mark Vainikka, national communications coordinator for the Assemblies of God in Australia, wrote, "The Church has to reach people who no longer believe that scientific rationalism, nor Christianity, has the answers to their problems. They don't believe in absolutes, they are knowledgeable and informed, uninterested in history, and place a lot of emphasis on relationships rather than hierarchy. According to many secular commentators, we have entered a 'post-Christian' and 'post-scientific' age."[2]

What can be done to strengthen
Sunday School in the local church?
"Make Sunday School the top priority."
—Lyle E. Schaller

The renewed focus on the importance of people teaching the Word of God is growing in intensity as boomers and generation Xers are coming back to church. There is a new hunger for knowing and learning the Word.

The Church must respond to this manifest need. We can and we will because the Sunday School is the network of small groups already in place just waiting to be energized and empowered by a pursuit of excellence in training and teaching. Most of these groups will probably meet on Sunday morning; however, as we will see, others are meeting at optional times that meet individual needs. Sunday School will survive because it is mission-driven—focused on people and God's Word.

The New Three Rs

The three Rs obviously bring to mind "reading, 'riting, and 'rithmetic." Many things occupy our minds with respect to the learning process; however, there is still the need for literacy in the fields of understanding, communication, and calculation.

In the realm of Sunday School ministries there is another category of Rs that come to mind—*reviewing, renewing,* and *resurgence.*

Reviewing. It is not good to dwell on the past. In fact, it is not always good to look back. Looking back can be costly—it cost Lot's wife her life. It can be disappointing and defeating; however, there are valuable lessons, if not encouragement, to be gained from proper times of review. Take a moment and review A. V. Washburn's Laws of Sunday School Growth for the 1920s:

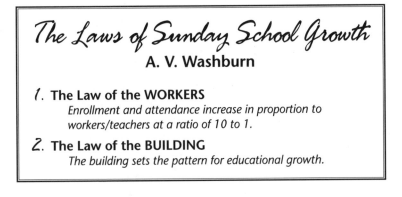

The Laws of Sunday School Growth
A. V. Washburn

1. **The Law of the WORKERS**
   Enrollment and attendance increase in proportion to workers/teachers at a ratio of 10 to 1.

2. **The Law of the BUILDING**
   The building sets the pattern for educational growth.

---

3. **The Law of NEW UNITS**

Sunday School units usually reach their maximum growth in a few months, therefore provide new classes for continued growth.

4. **The Law of GRADING**

Dividing students by ages/school grades provides the logical basis for adding new units.

5. **The Law of OUTREACH**

Enrollment and attendance increase in proportion to outreach and visitation.

In reviewing Sunday School, the points of perspective are vital. First, its history is profound. It continues to celebrate a great origin. Robert Raikes's vision for ministering to needy children is still relevant. The plan of taking Sunday School to the people is still a good plan. Second, Sunday School experienced a decline, the result of neglect or turning to other methods during the past 20 years. Third, agencies of concern have launched new efforts during recent years. These expressions of commitment have produced positive benefits.

Renewing. It is heartwarming to see the impact of renewed activity in the mission and purpose of Sunday School. The renewal of this movement to reach, teach, win, and care for people includes new attitudes among pastors, Sunday School superintendents, teachers, district leaders, and local church workers. Thousands of those workers have attended training seminars over the past few years.

Resurgence. Good things are happening. There is a new enthusiasm for outreach. There is a new attitude toward thinking more about people than about numbers. The results of such attitude changes are appearing in new growth patterns both in Sunday School and morning worship attendance. A new appreciation is emerging for the excellent ministry products available from Christian publishing houses. A strong partnership is forming between denominational agencies and pastors seen in a commitment that recognizes mutual dependence.

Yes, the three Rs are alive. These are great days for reviewing, renewing, and resurgence. People can be reached, taught, won to Christ, and cared for across generational lines through the Sunday School.

It Is Still the Good News

Each Christmas season, virtually the whole world stands still, believer and unbeliever, and reflects on the fact that something good happened on one special day 2,000 years ago.

The story will be told in thousands of ways, in thousands of languages—in churches, in public places, where allowed, and on private lawns with elaborate displays. Millions of Christmas lights will shine, televised programming will commemorate, special events will assemble festive gatherings, gifts will be exchanged: Christmas will again be the focal point of interest. And it should be!

Through it all comes the old, old story that His coming brought Good News to a bad-news world. Zechariah, father of John the Baptist, announced to the world that his son was to be named John and that he would "go ahead of the Master to prepare his ways" (Luke 1:76, TM).

He further declared that "God's Sunrise [daystar from on high] will break in upon us, shining on those in the darkness, those sitting in the shadow of death, then showing us the way, one foot at a time, down the path of peace" (vv. 78-79, TM). The language—whether in the familiar translations or the contemporary rendering of Eugene Peterson in *The Message*—makes it abundantly clear that His coming brought hope, life, light, and love to a desperate world that sat in darkness.

Today the world is bright with technology and travel. The world is connected through incredible means of communication. And yet, the citizens of this planet are victimized by present darkness and satanic influences.

Today there is hope: there is still the Good News that God's Sunrise has come, and He alone offers redemption and promise.

Today the challenge for the church and the mandate for *every Sunday School worker* is to be personally and corporately connected with the Dayspring from on high who still visits those who sit in darkness to bring salvation and to guide them in the way of peace.

What is the importance of Sunday Schools? Every teacher in every classroom has the opportunity both to find new joy in knowing Jesus Christ and to share that new joy with students.

A Teacher's Prayer

Each time before I face my class,
I hesitate awhile, and ask the Father,
"Help me, Lord, to understand each child,
Help me to see in every one a precious soul, most dear,
And may I lead that child through paths of wonder
—not of fear.
Dear Father, as they look to me for
Christian guidance true,
I look to You and humbly ask that
You will teach me, too."

—Anonymous

REDISCOVERY ACTION STEP
Heralding a New Vision for Sunday School

Every leader concerned about new growth through the Sunday School should prayerfully seek a new vision of its importance to the local church ministry. Vision casting may begin by answering several important ministry questions. First, "What are our past successes?" Knowing where you are going begins with a good look at where you have been. Hikers who reach the mountain summit get a clearer perspective of their progress by taking a look at the terrain they have successfully covered.

Second, "What is our present situation? What strengths do we have that can be utilized in a brand-new way for Sunday School ministry?" Likewise, another question may provide insight, "What weaknesses must we overcome to fill in the gaps and get us on the road to renewal?" Many times, an in-depth evaluation of your present ministry will be a source of encouragement, not discouragement. You may discover that you have been doing some of the right things. Don't fix the unbroken!

Third, "What should the future be? Where do we want to be in our Sunday School organization a year from now?" Factoring in facilities, staffing, equipment, finances, and the needs of the community, go before the Lord and ask Him to give you direction for revitalizing the Sunday School ministry in your local church.

There are at least seven important stages in vision planning:

1. Praying—relying on the resources God makes available to you

2. Understanding—looking at the emerging trends in today's society

3. Searching—asking, "Why do we have Sunday School?" (focusing on community needs)

4. Defining—asking, "What do we want to accomplish?" (defining the tasks to be accomplished)

5. Identifying—asking, "What is our common goal?" ([a] teach for edification, [b] teach for decision)

6. Processing—asking, "Is our Sunday School ministry effective?"

7. Reforming—making adjustments (keeping the vision current, checking the vital signs)

Rediscovering God's Word in the Sunday School

Assemble the people—men, women and children, and the aliens living in your towns—so they can listen and learn to fear the LORD your God and follow carefully all the words of this law.
(Deut. 31:12)

JAMES D. MURCH wrote, "Pure Christianity has always insisted on an educated consistuency—one that knows basic doctrine, why Christian beliefs are superior to other beliefs, that knows its basic ethical code and is intent on winning others to Christ." Biblical illiteracy is an alarming problem in the modern church. Itinerant evangelists say they often receive blank stares when they refer to familiar Bible stories (e.g., Daniel in the lions' den) in their sermons. Audience members often act as if they have never heard the story. A whole generation could be raised without the understanding of some of the basic stories of the Bible. The apostle Paul commented to Timothy, "From infancy you have known the holy Scriptures, which are able to make you wise for salvation through faith in Christ Jesus" (2 Tim. 3:15). Learning the Scriptures was a lifelong process in the education of Timothy.

In our move to need-based Christian education, a basic "user knowledge" of God's Word must not be overlooked. Phil Roberts wrote in *On Mission*, "Where the God of the Bible is worshipped, and His Son, the Lord Je-

"But first you have to agree to teach the
4-year-old Sunday School class!"

sus Christ is venerated, proclaimed lives are changed and
healthy vibrant congregations are built."[1]

We are drawn back to the desert road between
Jerusalem and Gaza where the apostle Philip met an offi-
cial from the court of Queen Candace. "On his way home
[the official] was sitting in his chariot reading the book of
Isaiah the prophet. The Spirit told Philip, 'Go to that chariot and stay near it.' . . . 'Do you understand what you are
reading?' Philip asked. 'How can I,' he said, 'unless someone explains it to me?'" (Acts 8:28-31).

Wake Up and Smell the Coffee!

A Sunday School teacher challenged her children to
take some time on Sunday afternoon to write a letter to
God. They were to bring back their letters the following
Sunday. One little boy wrote: "Dear God, We had a good
time at church today. Wish You would have been there."

The fact is, God is present at our gatherings! We must acknowledge His presence and power!

We have allowed ourselves to be so overwhelmed with the dimensions of our assignments and demographics that we have been lulled into a type of sleep. It makes us powerless to respond at a time when the cries of the world are appealing for a church that is wide awake.

We are being awakened to the problems and pain of a broken world. So, it is time to be awakened to the promises and power of the gospel. Just as the light of each new day brings life and opportunity, so an awakened church will receive the light of God.

A Christian leader awakened by a fresh encounter with God's Word will see his or her Christian work revived. Victorious living results from an awakened church whose believers are practicing Paul's advice to rely on heavenly resources, not human devices. "Do not get drunk on wine, which leads to debauchery. Instead, be filled with the Spirit. Speak to one another with psalms, hymns and spiritual songs. Sing and make music in your heart to the Lord" (Eph. 5:18-19).

A renewed emphasis on the Bible gives Sunday Schools an unlimited opportunity to experience new life and energy that will empower workers for effective ministry and service.

There is a new hunger for God. People haven't found lasting answers in the textbooks of their times. Seekers across ecclesiastical and cultural lines are crowding together into living rooms, classrooms, lunchrooms, and online chat rooms in a quest to know more about where planet Earth came from, how they arrived on it, and where they will be going when they leave it. It's an opportune time for the Church to guide them to the eternal truths of God's Word!

But those guides must not be blind guides. Christians must know the elementary principles of God's Word—until they can sing from their heart, "I stand alone on the

Word of God, the B-I-B-L-E." The time has come, in the life of the Church, for us to simply go back to the basics— *back to the Word!*

Five Ways to Emphasize the Bible in Sunday School

1. *Display it prominently.* When a student walks into the classroom, there should be no doubt that it is a place where God's Word is honored.

> These are the commands, decrees and laws the LORD your God directed me to teach you to observe in the land that you are crossing the Jordan to possess, so that you, your children and their children after them may fear the LORD your God as long as you live by keeping all his decrees and commands that I give you, and so that you may enjoy long life. Hear, O Israel, and be careful to obey so that it may go well with you and that you may increase greatly in a land flowing with milk and honey, just as the LORD, the God of your fathers, promised you. Hear, O Israel: The LORD our God, the LORD is one. Love the LORD your God with all your heart and with all your soul and with all your strength. These commandments that I give you today are to be upon your hearts. Impress them on your children. Talk about them when you sit at home and when you walk along the road, when you lie down and when you get up. Tie them as symbols on your hands and bind them on your foreheads. Write them on the doorframes of your houses and on your gates *(Deut. 6:1-9).*

God instructed that the devotion to His Word should result in its display. When the student walks into the classroom, there should be evidences of the Bible everywhere. From an open Bible at the front of the room to neatly written Scripture verses on wall posters, God's Word should be displayed prominently.

2. *Use it predominantly.* One group of New Testament Christians is commended for its emphasis on using the

Scriptures, "Now the Bereans were of more noble character than the Thessalonians, for they received the message with great eagerness and examined the Scriptures every day to see if what Paul said was true" (Acts 17:11). Their meetings were centered around their study of God's Word.

3. *Teach it practically.* Paul wrote, "He has made us competent as ministers of a new covenant—not of the letter but of the Spirit; for the letter kills, but the Spirit gives life" (2 Cor. 3:6). Students must see that God's Word is user-friendly. At every age level, the teaching of God's Word should result in opportunities to make life applications. Sunday School success depends on persons discovering that God's Word is alive and relevant in its "spirit" as well as its "letter."

4. *Discover it personally.* Sunday School leaders and workers cannot possibly emphasize the Bible in their ministry unless it is emphasized in their own lives. John advised, "This is the message we have heard from him and declare to you: God is light; in him there is no darkness at all" (1 John 1:5). The message the disciples declared was the message they experienced. A teaching ministry born out of a personal knowledge of God's Word is powerful and effective.

5. *Teach it proficiently.* The apostle Paul gave advice to all church workers through his words to Timothy, "Do your best to present yourself to God as one approved, a workman who does not need to be ashamed and who correctly handles the word of truth" (2 Tim. 2:15). Cutting-edge Sunday Schools can offer continuing education classes. Refresher courses on Old or New Testament books could prepare for an upcoming curriculum emphasis. For instance, if the quarterly curriculum focuses on the Ten Commandments, offer a refresher class on the Pentateuch to Sunday School workers beforehand. Use video, audio, or on-line teaching to familiarize workers with this portion of God's Word.

REDISCOVERY ACTION STEP
Building a World-Class Sunday School on the Word

Sunday School is a people-focused agency. Sunday School provides the greatest agency to demonstrate true love for people. In a world searching for truth, the Sunday School is the place where truth can be found in an atmosphere of loving concern.

Sunday School is a purpose-driven movement. One of the core values of the Sunday School is to *teach* God's Word to people.

Those who can, do. Those who can't, teach.

Give priority to *excellence* in Bible teaching methods. Give priority to *assimilating* new members. Track and study responses to Bible teaching in:

- Decisions
- First-time guests
- New partners in ministry
- Offerings
- Attendance

Give priority to *evaluating* Bible emphasis—

- "How do we measure up?"
- "Are we doing as well as we can?"
- "What adjustments need to be made?"

The Sunday School provides a unique opportunity to gain Bible knowledge and to study the applications of the Christian life to today's world.

—Charles Arn, Donald McGavran, and Win Arn

Rediscovering Evangelism
in the Sunday School

*The Lord added to their number daily those
who were being saved.*
(Acts 2:47)

A MAN WAS STRANDED on the proverbial deserted Pacific island for years. Finally one day a boat came sailing into view, and the man frantically waved and drew the skipper's attention. The boat came near the island and the sailor came ashore and greeted the stranded man.

Quizzically the sailor asked, "What are those three huts you have here?"

"Well, the first one is my house," answered the lonely man.

"What's the second hut?" asked the sailor.

"I built that hut to be my church," replied the stranded man.

The sailor continued to interrogate, "And the other hut?"

The man responded, "Oh, that's where I used to go to church."

Sadly, transfer growth seems to be the outreach tool of the day for many churches. It is now time for the church to make evangelism an essential priority.

Sunday Schools are not exempt from the Great Commission. The last words of Christ are the first words to the Sunday School intent on revival: "Then Jesus came to them and said, 'All authority in heaven and on earth has been given to me. Therefore go and make disciples of all nations, baptizing them in the name of the Father and of the Son and of the Holy Spirit, and teaching them to obey everything I have commanded you. And surely I am with you always, to the very end of the age'" (Matt. 28:18-20).

The old adage "The main thing is to keep the main thing the main thing" is especially relevant to evangelism in the Sunday School. The *main thing* for Sunday Schools is to carry out the Great Commission to children, youth, and adults in preparation for a lifetime of Christian holiness.

Sunday School is about connections, vertical and horizontal. It is the connecting link between people whose lives have been changed and assimilated into the Body of Christ and people who are in need of the Savior and identification with the community of the redeemed.

Sunday School is being rediscovered as the small-group method of choice for carrying out the Great Commission that offers a simple plan for people connecting with people. The Great Commission itself offers a design that provides workable strategies that are balanced in concept and structure. The *main thing* (the Great Commission) has three dimensions:

- Going—evangelism

- Baptizing—assimilating

- Teaching—discipleship

Sunday School is about the *main thing* because it is grounded in the Great Commission. Pastors, Sunday School superintendents, teachers, workers, one and all, are called to carefully, prayerfully, and effectively "keep the main thing the main thing"—*because it is the main thing!*

An unknown author penned this paraphrase of 1 Cor. 13:

Though I speak with the tongues of scholarship, and though I use approved methods of education, and fail to win my pupils to Christ, I become as a cloud of mist in an open sea, as the moan of the wind in a Syrian desert.

And though I read all Sunday School literature, and attend Sunday School conventions and institutes and summer schools, and yet am satisfied with less than winning to Christ and establishing my pupils in Christian character and service, it profiteth me nothing.

The soul-winning teacher, the character-building teacher suffereth long and is kind; he envieth not others who are free from the teaching task; he vaunteth not himself, is not puffed up with intellectual pride.

Such a teacher doth not behave unseemingly between Sundays, seeketh not his own comfort, is not easily provoked.

Beareth all things, believeth all things, hopeth all things.

And now abideth knowledge, methods, evangelism, these three; but the greatest of these is evangelism.

A core value of the Sunday School is winning people to Christ.

The "Go" Factor

It could be said that without the letters *g-o* there is no *growth*. Billy Graham once wrote, "One of the greatest hindrances to evangelism today is the poverty of our own experience in evangelism." The *outreach* challenge for the Sunday School is ever before us. But the danger is that the concept has been so ingrained in our thinking that we view it more as a program than a passion to carry out Christ's final word to those who followed Him.

True, *go* is the word Jesus spoke to His band of followers. However, long before He came to earth, the strategy of the Godhead was to establish and advance a spiritual kingdom. "For he chose us in him before the creation of the world to be holy and blameless in his sight" (Eph. 1:4).

Evangelism is to bear witness to the gospel with soul aflame and to teach and preach with the express purpose of making disciples of those who hear.

—C. E. Autry

Sunday School Is the Growth Tool of the Future

The Sunday School is an opportune place to present the claims of the gospel. Dr. Ken Hemphill, author of the book *Revitalizing the Sunday Morning Dinosaur*, suggests eight reasons why Sunday School is the *growth tool* of the future. Let's look at those reasons in the context of Sunday School evangelism.

1. *Sunday School provides a centralized and simplified strategy.* The Sunday School can be organized in a way that focuses on evangelism. Through "Decision Sundays," gospel presentation events, media, membership training classes, and so forth, the gospel can be presented in a nonthreatening, caring environment.

2. *Sunday School is familiar.* Sunday School is a great environment for building relationships with the unchurched. Most of the people who walk through the doors of your church have had some past exposure to Sunday School. Early in their childhood they may have been taken to Sunday School—and that experience most likely brings fond remembrances to their minds.

3. *Sunday School is a solid foundation for innovation.* Sunday School is a great atmosphere for introducing new methods of sharing Christ. It is a "safe environment" and the presenters are, for the most part, familiar to the attendees. The "old message" can be presented in a fresh new way without intimidation.

4. *Sunday School is the natural companion to an exciting worship service.* If people in your community are more likely to come first to a worship service, the Sunday

School still provides the best method for assimilating these newcomers so that they become attached to the family.

5. *Sunday School gets people involved in service.* Sunday School is a great place to share your faith. The rapport that is established between workers and attendees makes it more likely for them to grant that worker permission to present Christ.

6. *Sunday School provides the small-group experience every Christian needs.* Spontaneous personal testimonies given in a small-group setting often have a greater impact on seekers than a well-prepared sermon. The seeker will likely be drawn by the faith-in-action words of a committed Christian. Plus, involvement in a small group says, "You are wanted; you belong." It provides a "safe" place for expressing spiritual needs and enlisting the support of other Christians for spiritual growth.

7. *Sunday School is not tied to a single personality.* Personalities come and go, but the permanence of the Sunday School structure is inviting to seekers. Many of those hungry hearts have been turned off by the failures of ministry "personalities."

Sunday School is an ideal place to form genuine friendships. The continuing interaction of teacher to student, and student to student, based on authentic Christianity can override many negative attitudes toward the church.

8. *Sunday School has a proven track record.* Many of your church attenders were introduced to Christ through the Sunday School. Most Sunday School workers will respond favorably to a Sunday School evangelism program because they know how important that ministry was in their own conversion.[1]

Sunday School Evangelists and Evangelistic Sunday Schools

Bill Hybels says that 10 percent of the people in your church have the spiritual gift of evangelism. Someone defined that gift as the "ability to lead people beyond their own natural sphere of influence to a saving knowledge of Jesus Christ. In the exercise of this gift, the evangelist is the aggressive soul winner who seeks the lost. The strengths of this gift include: (1) a consuming passion for lost souls, (2) a clear understanding of the gospel and what it can do in one's life, and (3) a desire to improve effectiveness through Scripture memory." Peter Wagner says, "Evangelism is seeking and finding the lost, effectively presenting the gospel to them, and persuading them to become Christ's disciples, responsible members of His church."

Everyone in your Sunday School may not be a Spirit-gifted evangelist, but everyone in your Sunday School can be involved in a Spirit-empowered evangelistic movement. John Stott wrote, "Evangelism means announcing or proclaiming the good news of Jesus." Cutting-edge Sunday Schools will be doing just that!

The 1st-century church is the model for the 21st century, "A great persecution broke out against the church at Jerusalem, and all except the apostles were scattered throughout Judea and Samaria. . . . Those who had been scattered preached the word wherever they went" (Acts 8:1, 4). The "evangelists" were in Jerusalem, but the "evangelistic movement" was happening wherever the church was located.

Twenty-First Century Evangelism Challenges

1. Sunday Schools must face the challenge of a new spiritual openness. A *USA Today* study, reported in *On Mission*, compared today's adults with those of 1976. It found a "spiritually open America."

	1976	1999
Believe in spiritualism	12%	52%
Believe in astrology	17%	37%
Believe in reincarnation	9%	25%
Believe in faith healing	10%	45%
Believe in UFOs	24%	30%[2]

2. Sunday Schools must face the challenge of a changing society:

By 2020, there will be 130 million Hispanics living in America and only 2 percent of them will be Protestant Christians.

By 2020, there will be 70 million Islamic followers in America with one goal—to make an Islamic nation.

By 2020, 42 percent of the United States will be single.

By 2020, 52 percent of the United States will be over 50.

By 2020, native-born Americans will be in the minority.

By 2020, there will be more missionaries coming into the United States than going out.

—George Gallup Polls

3. Sunday Schools must face the challenge of evangelism "barriers":

 a. The Attitude Barrier. Like a computer, many churches are in a "sleep mode." Their evangelistic "system" has automatically shut down due to inactivity. They need to "boot up" to the great potential for reaching and winning people to Christ through the Sunday School.

 b. The Behavior Barrier. Many churches are not extending their hand to the unchurched—and the unchurched are becoming increasingly distant. The church must be taught how to put out the "red carpet" for people in their community who need someone to care about them.

 c. The Knowledge Barrier. Many churches lack a basic understanding of Christ's Great Commission. The church needs to understand that Christ's call is not optional, that no organizational structure is viable without an ultimate purpose of leading people to the Savior.

 d. The Methods Barrier. Many Christians have not been trained to share their faith—they just don't know how. A simple plan of salvation can be taught that may result in a host of people coming to know Christ.

The ABCs of a
Personal Relationship with Christ:

Receiving Jesus Christ is as simple as ABC . . .

Admit that you have sinned.   Romans 3:23

Believe that Jesus Christ died for you.   John 1:12

Confess that Jesus Christ is Lord of your life.   Romans 10:9

"Dear God, I know that I am a sinner. I believe that You died for my sins and arose from the grave. I now turn from my sins and invite You to come into my heart and life. I receive You as my personal Savior and follow You as my Lord. Amen."   —Stan Toler[3]

Michael Green said in his book *Evangelism in the Early Church,* "If there is one God, Creator, Redeemer, Judge, as the early church passionately asserted, then those who have been brought back from their rebellion against Him into fellowship with Him cannot but pass on the knowledge of that rescue to others; the new life cries out to be shared."[4]

The words of the Master ring even clearer today, "Do you not say, 'Four months more and then the harvest'? I tell you, open your eyes and look at the fields! They are ripe for harvest" (John 4:35).

I believe in Sunday School because it is a tried and
proven, time tested, life changing, chronological,
systematic method of teaching the whole Bible
as the Word of God to all ages.

—Bennie Triplett

"YES!" to the Great Commission

Say *yes* to the Great Commission, to the priorities of Christ and His Church, to rediscovery of the Word, to the vision of Kingdom expansion, to caring for people.

Say *yes* to a system that provides an organizational structure of small, manageable groups designed to care for people, to facilitate biblical learning, to assimilate them into the church family.

How to Keep Evangelism at the Center of Your Small Group

- Empty chair. Keep an empty chair at each meeting to represent someone you would like to bring into the group.
- Prospect list. Make a prospect list with names of people, both outside and inside the church, who need to be in a group.
- Social evening. Start a new group by having a social evening and inviting all the people on a prospect list.
- Reporting. Ask group leaders to regularly fill out a short report that asks how many newcomers they are reaching.
- Baptisms. When new converts are baptized, ask their small-group leader to stand alongside the pastor as a witness.
- Lessons. Regularly include questions that deal with becoming a new Christian.
- Acts of kindness. Small acts of kindness earn the right to invite people to a friendship group.
- Reproduction. Build the idea of reproduction into the DNA of each group by putting an apprentice in place when a group is started.
- Leadership training. Teach leaders how to lead someone to Christ.
- New groups. Create new groups that target needs and interests.

—Dale Galloway[5]

Say *yes* to equipping people for lay ministry and corporate evangelism.

Say *yes* to footholds and beachheads established by visionary believers working daily in hand-to-hand combat against the enemy of human souls; *yes* to the unleashed power of purpose-driven workers, knocking on doors of absentees, prospects, and other Sunday School members.

Say *yes* to the power of God's Word to redraw the frontiers of vision in every local Sunday School and church.

Answering the Call to Care

Recently, a friend of the author's traded his vehicle for another car. During the transaction, he mentioned that he worked at the Church of the Nazarene's International Headquarters. The salesperson reacted by telling him about a neighbor, a layperson in the Church of the Nazarene, who reached out to the salesperson when he was a 12-year-old child struggling with the meaning of a broken home.

Every Sunday morning the neighbor would take him to Sunday School. Not content to end his involvement there, the neighbor became involved in the boy's life. For instance, when the boy missed his ride to a scout camp, he took him to meet the scoutmaster. After long days on the job, the neighbor pounded the driveway, dribbling basketballs and playing pickup games with his kids and the 12-year-old neighbor.

The call to reaching people and winning them to Christ begins with answering the call to care. That 12-year-old is now a member of a local church—because someone answered the call.

Next door, around the corner, in the next office—are people who need to know that we care enough about them to introduce them to Jesus Christ.

REDISCOVERY ACTION STEP
Mobilizing the Sunday School for Evangelism

1. Start with strategic planning.
   - Gather your leaders together for prayer, asking God to give you a vision for soul-winning in the Sunday School.
   - Research and discuss some emerging trends.
   - Evaluate your ministry capabilities. What are the strengths and weaknesses that may help or hinder your evangelism emphasis?
   - Define what you want to accomplish during your evangelism emphasis.
   - Inventory your resources (financial, personnel, facilities, materials).
   - Develop a plan (theme, dates, action steps, etc.).

2. Mobilize the laity.
   - Develop a churchwide prayer involvement (day of prayer, prayer chain, etc.).
   - Promote the theme/emphasis through your local church publications and announcements.
   - Gather materials (soul-winning training, outreach materials, follow-up).
   - Offer training in the presentation of a salvation plan.
   - Give public recognition of workers who have completed the training.

3. Launch your evangelism emphasis.
   - Target specific people groups:
     - Age-specific (children, youth, adults, senior adults)
     - Need-specific (single, young married, divorced)
     - Ministry-specific (first-time visitors, absentees, neighborhood)
   - Plan and launch evangelism events/opportunities:
     - Decision days

- Concerts
- Short-term classes
- New classes
- Neighborhood activities
- Need-specific seminars/classes

4. Strategically plan to follow up on new converts.
   - Distribute follow-up materials.
   - Assign prayer partners/mentors.
   - Offer new Christian/pastor classes.
   - Plan fellowship activities.

Rediscovering Organization in the Sunday School

Do not those who plot evil go astray?
But those who plan what is good find love and faithfulness.
(Prov. 14:22)

PERHAPS YOU'VE HEARD the story about the pastor who went to his church office on Monday morning and discovered a dead mule. After much thought he decided to call the local sheriff. Since there did not appear to be any foul play, the sheriff recommended that the pastor call the local health authorities.

The health director indicated that there was no immediate health threat and told him to call the sanitation department. The sanitation director told him that he could not pick up the mule without authorization from the mayor.

Unfortunately, the pastor knew the mayor and was not excited about calling him. The mayor had a bad temper and was known to be difficult to deal with.

Finally, the pastor mustered the courage to call the mayor. The mayor immediately began to rant and rave and finally said, "Why did you call me anyway? Isn't it your job to bury the dead?"

The pastor, collecting his thoughts, paused for a brief prayer and asked the Lord to direct his response. He then said, "Mayor, it is my job to bury the dead, but I always like to notify the next of kin first!"

The story about the pastor and the mule illustrates the problems we often encounter in dealing with governmental agencies. But, it also reminds us that the Sunday School was never intended to be a red-tape, rules-keeping organization. It was designed to be easy to join and highly relational.

Structuring for Sunday School Growth

It is important for Sunday School leaders to understand that sanctified "structure" is vital to effectiveness. Christian A. Schwarz wrote in *Natural Church Development: A Guide to Eight Essential Qualities of Healthy Churches:*

> One of the biggest barriers to recognizing the significance of structures for church development is the widespread view that "structure" and "life" are opposites. Interestingly enough, biological research reveals that dead matter and living organisms are not distinguished by their substance, as some people might think, but by the specific structure of the relationship of the individual parts to each other . . . This intimate connection between structure and life was first expressed at creation. The act of creation was an act of forming and shaping . . . Wherever God breathes His Spirit into formless clay, both life and form spring forth. A comparative creative act occurs wherever God pours out His Spirit within the church today—and thus giving it structure and form.[1]

Sunday School architects will keep the foundation, but the structure may need some improvement. Structure doesn't cause Sunday School growth, but it does affect the rate and size of its growth.

Dr. J. K. Warrick, pastor of the College Church of the Nazarene in Olathe, Kansas, is an outstanding promoter and organizer of adult Sunday Schools. Pastor Warrick, Sunday School Superintendent David Caudle, and Associate Pastor Dan Vanderpool organize Adult Bible Study Fellowship in the following manner:

ADULT BIBLE STUDY FELLOWSHIP ORGANIZATION

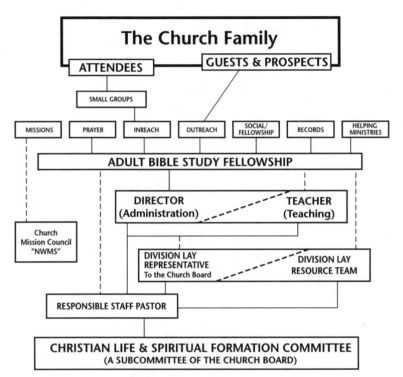

The College Church team also meets monthly to deal with all aspects of the Adult Bible Study Fellowship organization. Here's a sample plan of action:

MONTHLY PLANNING FOR ACTION MEETING
Olathe College Church of the Nazarene
J. K. Warrick, Pastor

WHO ATTENDS: Leadership Team of each Adult Bible Study Fellowship

WHY: To plan, evaluate for an effective, growing Bible Study Fellowship

WHEN: On a designated Wednesday evening each month during
   7:00—8:00 hour
WHERE: Room S-115 (West of the North Sanctuary Lobby)

AGENDA

General Division Meeting
Class Leaders Meeting

—The Bible Study Fellowship director chairs the meeting.

—The inreach coordinator reports on the nature of group members' absences and efforts made to contact them.

—The records coordinator reports those that need to be added to or deleted from the responsibility list.

—The social coordinator reports on plans for class social times both inside and outside of the Sunday hour.

—The mission education coordinator reports on number of missionary books read, missions education emphasis Sundays; LINKS missionary family involvement; Work and Witness project.

—The outreach coordinator reports on visitors' attendance and follow-up from the follow-up file, as well as those prospects from the church office.

—The helping ministries coordinator reports on helping response for the month.

—The prayer coordinator reports on plans for prayer involvement both inside and outside the ABSF hour.

—The teacher assists the ABSF Leadership Team in regular evaluation and planning during Planning for Action meetings.

Building Blocks to Restructure the Sunday School

There are several important building blocks that will help to restructure the Sunday School:

Building Block No. 1: *Simplify the organization and structure.*

Arthur Flake was a true pioneer in the American Sunday School movement. He was in the pattern of Robert Raikes, the layperson in England who founded the Sunday School.

A successful businessman and traveling salesman, Mr.

Flake started a department store business in Winona, Mississippi. According to Sunday School leader Dr. Billy Taylor, Flake was Sunday School superintendent at Winona Baptist Church. "Using his business acumen, he studied the Sunday School and its needs and developed the practical methods that have so completely revolutionized Sunday School work." He is known across denominational lines for providing the Flake Formula. It has been shared in various ways; however, its five essential components may be used in organizing Sunday School ministries. They are:

1. Locate the Prospects
2. Enlarge the Organization (add a class)
3. Recruit and Train the Workers
4. Provide the Space
5. Go After the People

—Arthur Flake

Can a formula that is virtually a century old have any value today? Obviously, the Flake Formula will work today if it is applied. Identifying and focusing on essentials is a good place to start when analyzing your organization and structure.

The essentials, identified in the Flake Formula, form the girders on which the entire Sunday School "building" is supported. Without them, all the "floors," "rooms," and "equipment" will be jeopardized. Organizing around the basic purpose of the Sunday School gives it strength.

Peter Wagner said in his book *The Healthy Church,* "It is recommended that a church carefully examine the needs of the unchurched people around it, establish a philosophy of ministry that will meet those needs and plan to grow until it is large enough to conduct that sort of ministry adequately."[2] It is a primary observation but essential to long-term effectiveness in Sunday School ministries. Start with a simple plan for meeting needs and let the organization grow accordingly.

The church must be both culturally relevant and
socially sensitive. It should base its ministries
on evident needs and find a balance between
both evangelism and edification.
—Michael Anthony

Building Block No. 2: *Build a winning team.*

The Sunday School organization must identify and recruit leaders. In that recruitment process, leadership qualities need to be identified. These include:

- Vision that looks beyond the present
- Integrity that characterizes lifestyle
- Risk-taking when others shrink back
- Patience that equalizes the pressures that occur
- Kindness that binds people together as a golden chain

The Sunday School leadership must not only be
trained but also, in turn, become responsible for training
others. The focus of Sunday School leadership should be
on a systematic equipping of workers. The apostle Paul
modeled this "training chain" theory in his advice to Pastor Timothy, "And the things you have heard me say in
the presence of many witnesses entrust to reliable men
who will also be qualified to teach others" (2 Tim. 2:2).

Why have training sessions?

First, because of the need for information. Every successful organization has a constant and consistent flow of
form, fact, and philosophy that keeps the organization on
its predetermined course. It's no different for the Sunday
School. Every worker needs to be acquainted with the
Sunday School's purpose (philosophy), be advised of current data (fact), and given appropriate materials (form) to
help keep it on course.

© 1997 Dik Lapine

"I asked for new nursery furniture.
Guess I didn't say what kind of nursery."

Second, because of the need for instruction. Forms, facts, and philosophies are meaningless unless they can be practically applied to the lives of students. Every teacher needs to know how to present God's truth in a clearly understandable way. If public schoolteachers need hands-on training to teach secular principles, how much more does the Sunday School teacher need training to teach eternal principles!

Third, because of the need for involvement. Training sessions allow for a time of sharing purpose and ideas. What may not be learned in a formal classroom may be learned in an informal discussion time. For example, the "veteran" teacher may have just the right technique for discipline in the classroom that a "rookie" teacher will pick up in a discussion of classroom conduct.

Fourth, because of the need for inspiration. The athletic team "huddle" is not only a time when plays are called but also a time when encouragement is given. There is an excitement that results from "getting together" during the "game" for a time of reflection, instruction, and motivation. Training sessions offer that same kind of inspiration.

Building Block No. 3: *Focus on changed lives.*

People are the reason for teaching. Ruth Vaughn Kaul says, "Teaching is a partnership with God. You are not molding iron nor chiseling marble: you are working with the Creator of the universe in shaping human character and determining destiny."[3]

Good teaching requires a minimum of three things:

> *A Bible.* God's Word must be at the center of any education offered by a Sunday School teacher! Just as the pastor is a person of the Book from the pulpit, the teacher is a person of the Book in the classroom.
>
> *A love for people.* The teacher sees each person as someone on a journey to eternity. The task of the teacher is to encourage interest in godliness and spiritual things through good teaching, personal motivation, and most of all, a loving example. When students leave the classroom, the love of the leader should be remembered as well as the lesson!
>
> *A desire to grow.* Sharpening the skills of teaching is a major priority for growing teachers. They realize there must be continual training if there is to be growth in the classroom—and growth on a personal level.

The law of the teacher: "If you stop growing today, you stop teaching tomorrow." Neither personality nor methodology can substitute for this principle. You cannot communicate out of a vacuum. You cannot impart what you do not possess. If you don't know it—truly know it—you can't give it. This law embraces the philosophy that I, as a teacher, am primarily a learner.

—Howard Hendricks

A New Organizational Paradigm

Youngsters enjoy putting models together—airplanes, cars, ships. Those models come with directions that assist the builder in putting the pieces of the model together.

Modern society has coined a word for its models: paradigms.

In regard to Sunday School organization, a new paradigm is needed if it is to continue to succeed into the future. Consider the following organizational steps in your evaluation and planning:

Step One: Optional classes should be offered.

We live in an age of options—the remote-control age. TV broadcasters know the importance of giving the viewer a reason to stay tuned because he or she has so many other possibilities—hundreds of satellite and cable channels. Studies show that, most likely, the viewer will change channels every 15 minutes. Cutting-edge Sunday Schools will capitalize on providing Spirit-led, multiple learning options for students.

The Sunday School can offer options not only in subject matter—marriage, finances, divorce recovery, and more—but also in the location of class sessions. For example, some Sunday Schools are meeting off-campus in local coffee shops, fast-food restaurants, shopping malls, and so forth.

Step Two: Establish a caring system.

Four words describe the pastoral care process:

▶ CARE

Cutting-edge Sunday Schools will be concerned with the constant care of their people—and that pastoral care philosophy will be included in the organizational structure. Again, Paul advised, "Preach the Word; be prepared in season and out of season; correct, rebuke and encourage—with great patience and careful instruction" (2 Tim. 4:2).

Sunday School students are on a spiritual journey. Leaders and workers have the opportunity to provide guideposts for the journey. Those guideposts include:

- Prayer. Leaders and workers have the opportunity to pray daily for their responsibility list—and let those people know about it.

In my experience, the deeper one's prayer life is, the deeper one's commitment to Christ and the deeper one's love for others.

—Sheila Manchester

A general sense of prayerlessness has tragically invaded the Kingdom. One study by Peter Wagner quoted in *Good News* magazine (May-June 1999) revealed that "most U.S. pastors pray fewer than 30 minutes a day."[4] If that is true of vocational ministers, what must the prayer journals of lay ministers reveal?

Prayer is Kingdom-focused, as seen in the Lord's Prayer, "This is how you should pray: 'Our Father in heaven, hallowed be your name, your kingdom come, your will be done on earth as it is in heaven'" (Matt. 6:9-10). God's kingdom comes clearly into focus when we pray. His will becomes primary. Relationships are clearly defined. Lifestyles are viewed in His light. His glory becomes the passion of the heart. Life is viewed in the light of eternal implications.

- Building relationships. Get to know people by name. Be able to identify Sunday School students when you see them downtown or bump into them at the mall. Take time to learn about their family. Learn to be a friend!

- Looking out for needs. Leaders must always be on the alert for those in their organization who need some TLC. Some may try to hide it more than others, but ask God to give you a spiritual sensitivity. A call or note within 24 hours can bring a wealth of encouragement to those who need it most.

Also, check your responsibility list for absentees, and make personal contact. It's a good rule to never let a week go by without contacting at least one person.

- Making goodwill gestures. Secular organizations know the importance of distributing tangible expressions of goodwill. Whole companies are formed for the sole purpose of manufacturing gifts with inscribed trademarks or logos for corporations or organizations to give to current or potential clients. Your Sunday School may not have the budget for purchasing from the same catalogs as secular organizations, but goodwill gift giving can be creatively utilized. Baked goods (bread, cookies, pies, etc.); a cup filled with candy and a picture of your church on it; or a flower arrangement are examples of goodwill gifts that can be given to prospects and visitors as a tangible expression of your caring.

▶ PREPARE

Paul S. Rees once said, "Visions are born of care and are given form and substance through added preparation."

- Be prepared mentally. The Sunday School teacher, for example, anticipates the questions students will ask. If a question cannot be answered, a promise to do further research is delivered. Washington Irving said, "It is in knowledge as in swimming; he who flounders and splashes on the surface makes more noise and attracts more attention than the pearl diver who quietly dives in quest of treasures at the bottom."

- Be prepared administratively. An effective leader . . .
    - *builds* relationships with others
    - *understands* the power of fellowship
    - *seeks* the collective wisdom of the organization
    - *accepts* pain and disappointment in stride
    - *never stops* reading
    - *attends* conferences, workshops, and seminars[5]
- Be prepared informatively. One key to effective organization is communication. Sunday School leaders and workers should cultivate the art of communication. They will express their thoughts with confidence after thorough research. They will use humor to keep the crowd alert. They will seek to understand their audience. They will speak with clarity.

▶ SHARE

The new Sunday School will be creative through Spirit-led innovation. People need to be spiritually motivated, and the organizational leader's job is to introduce those things that motivate them. The primary "motivators," however, are basic to Christian faith: God's love, God's forgiveness, God's promises.

A Christlike vision for reaching the unchurched and caring for the "churched" is understood best in the context of the interests, needs, and desires of those we serve, so that they may better know Jesus.

Unless we can and do constantly seek and find ways and means to do a better job; unless we accept the challenge of the changing times; we have no right to survive and we shall not survive.

—Chester O. Fisher

▶ DARE

1. Invite people. From the millionaire to the street person, invite people who don't usually get invited to Sunday School. Only 30 percent of Americans attend church on any given Sunday. What a wonderful opportunity we have to contact the 70 percent not attending!

2. Instruct people. Let the Sunday School be the place where a clear presentation of the gospel is given. Let the Sunday School be a place where core values are learned in the context of God's Word. Let the Sunday School be a place where eternal truths are shared in the light of temporal responsibilities.

3. Involve people. Get people involved in ministry. No matter how small the assignment, a shared vision for ministry begins with a shared work. Part of the assimilation process is assigning people to tasks that make them feel like they are a part of the organization.

4. Inspire people. Let people know what God has to offer them. In an impersonal world, people need to know what a personal relationship

with God will do in their lives. Talk about Jesus! He is the model for successful living. Tell about His birth, life, death, and victory over the grave. Use the personal testimonies of people who have walked with Him to motivate those who are learning how to walk with Him.

Little Things Mean So Much

In a world captivated by grandeur and immensity, it is somewhat paradoxical to suggest that "little things mean a lot." Perhaps in a world of sight, imagery, and sound, it is strange to think about small things having any real significance.

The Book of Proverbs (30:24-28) gives us a word picture of small things that proclaim mighty truths and principles:

Four things on earth are small, yet they are extremely wise: Ants are creatures of little strength, yet they store up their food in the summer; coneys [rock badgers] are creatures of little power, yet they make their home in the crags; locusts have no king, yet they advance together in ranks; a lizard can be caught with the hand, yet it is found in kings' palaces.

There is much for the organizational leader to learn from these small creatures:

1. Time is a precious commodity. It is valued. It is to be respected. It is uncertain. It is fleeting. It provides opportunity. It has an ending.

2. Safety in Him is available. It is promised. It is provided. It is enough. It is rewarding. It is inspiring. It motivates.

3. Unity is possible. Locusts offer incredible hope through a tactical procedure. Unity is an imperative. Togetherness is essential. Moving in ranks suggests mutual dependence.

4. Shelter is promised. Presence in the house of the King is available to the small and to the great.

Our small efforts in organizing the Sunday School to teach, win, and care for people results in large—and eternal—rewards.

REDISCOVERY ACTION STEP
Determining Spiritual Goals for the Sunday School Organization

The church at Antioch is a model for goal-setting (Acts 11:19-26; 13:1-4):

1. Set goals for WITNESSING. They "began to speak to Greeks also, telling them the good news about the Lord Jesus" (11:20).

2. Set goals for SOUL WINNING. "The Lord's hand was with them, and a great number of people believed and turned to the Lord" (11:21).

3. Set goals for TEACHING. "For a whole year, Barnabas and Saul met with the church and taught great numbers of people. The disciples were called Christians first at Antioch" (11:26).

4. Set goals for GIVING. "The disciples, each according to his ability, decided to provide help for the brothers living in Judea" (11:29).

5. Set goals for WORSHIPING. "While they were worshiping the Lord and fasting, the Holy Spirit said, 'Set apart for me Barnabas and Saul for the work to which I have called them'" (13:2).

6. Set goals for PRAYING. "After they had fasted and prayed . . ." (13:3).

7. Set goals for SENDING. "They placed their hands on them and sent them off" (13:3).

The result: "The Lord's hand was with them, and a great number of people believed and turned to the Lord" (Acts 11:21).

Rediscovering Fellowship in the Sunday School

We proclaim to you what we have seen and heard, so that you also may have fellowship with us. And our fellowship is with the Father and with his Son, Jesus Christ.
(1 John 1:3)

A YOUNG COUPLE came to a local church through a Bible study. When the study concluded, the young woman continued to attend a Sunday School class. The husband, an unbeliever, joined her occasionally.

One Sunday, the hospitality chairman of her Sunday School class opened the floor for prayer requests. The wife decided to share with her class something that was weighing heavily on her heart.

She explained that her husband had just discovered structural damage in the house they'd purchased a year earlier. The problem had been hidden by the former owners and would cost over $20,000 to repair. She explained that she didn't know where to begin to find a contractor, and besides, the couple was already deep in debt.

The next day, the Sunday School class leader, a contractor, visited the young couple to see how he could help. Soon other class members made commitments. The local pastor contacted a lawyer friend for legal advice. Hearing the plight of the couple, the attorney agreed to represent them with his salary contingent upon winning the case.

Others pitched in—donating dollars along with encouragement. Later, the husband was asked by fellow workers if he needed some help.

"No, thanks," he replied. "Our church is already taking care of us."

Fellowship is more than attending a Sunday School class with other members. It is getting involved in their lives—with tangible gifts: words of support, time, and talent.

Fellowship Is "Caring-ship"

Lyle E. Schaller once wrote, "While some church shoppers, especially those who live alone, and those who were born before 1935, place friendliness at the top of their list in evaluating churches, the vast majority place another criterion at the top: Does this congregation appear to be one that will be relevant and responsive to my religious needs? In other words, 'Do they really care about me?'"[1]

Jesus modeled "caring-ship." He loved people where they were regardless of who they were. He loved children, "He took the children in his arms, put his hands on them and blessed them" (Mark 10:16). He also loved the youth. The encounter with the rich young ruler is given in the context of His love. The words are very clear, "Jesus looked at him and loved him" (Mark 10:21). And the Bible gives us countless examples of Jesus showing concern, compassion, and love for adults of all ages.

The rediscovery of fellowship (caring-ship) in the Sunday School is the rediscovery of God's love in relation to our ministry as leaders and workers. What would happen if once again we were known as the church, the preacher, the superintendent, the teacher, or the individual who *really cares about people*? Our greatest need is to be the love connection that links a hungry, hurting world with Christ.

Sunday School members can practice their caringship in many ways:

- Listening—Sometimes all a person needs to feel loved is a listening ear.

- Noticing—Train yourself to be observant. Notice when someone is absent and, without nagging, let the person know he or she was missed. Notice unusual signs of distress—or elation—and ask.

- Speaking—Say, "How are you?" and really mean it. Give the person room to honestly tell you.

- Being hospitable—Be the first to make friendship moves. Invite someone to dinner, volunteer to help with a need, and so on.

- Remembering prayer requests—Ask about the outcome later.

- Encouraging—Give verbal affirmations.

- Interceding—Take time to pray with them.

- Being there—Visit people in the hospital. Attend events that are special to them, just because you care. Simply be there for them when they need you.

- Writing—Send a note—but not just when you know something is wrong. Write a note of encouragement, affirmation, let someone know you really care.

Calvary Church of the Nazarene in Bethany, Oklahoma, does an excellent job of making people feel welcome. Several years ago, under the leadership of layperson Harry Miller, the "Seven Touches of Calvary" was established. Today, the program is continued with excellence under the watchful eye of Pastor Larry Pruitt.

The following diagram describes the flow of "Seven Touches of Calvary":

SEVEN TOUCHES OF CALVARY

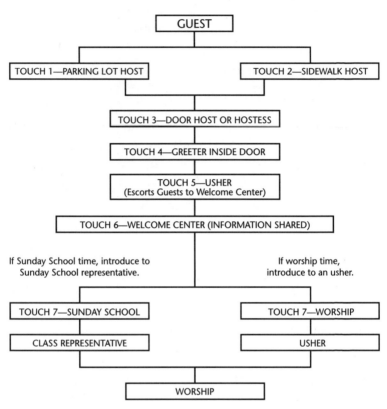

—Harry Miller

Seven Touches of Calvary "Follow-up"	
TOUCH 1 An Expression of Love: "Love Loaves"	Guests receive a loaf of bread
TOUCH 2 A Word of Appreciation: "Phone Ministry"	Every Sunday School and morning worship visitor receives a phone call Sunday afternoon
TOUCH 3 A Letter of Appreciation: "Pastor and Staff"	A letter from pastor welcoming the visitors to our fellowship

TOUCH 4 A Ministry of Outreach: "Sunday School outreach"	Every Sunday School class makes contact with the visitor
TOUCH 5 A Ministry of Love/Acceptance: "A ministry of friendship"	Families at Calvary invite guests into their homes for a meal
TOUCH 6 A Ministry of Involvement: "Special groups"	Involving new people in special groups
TOUCH 7 A Time of Fellowship: "Friendship night"	An evening of fellowship with those who have visited our fellowship

—Harry L. Miller
Used by permission

"Body Count?" or "Body Life?"

One pastor tells of his first Sunday School rally day. As a young pastor, he had visions of filling the auditorium of the staid old city church. He mustered enough nerve to set a goal of 200 for the anticipated day. Soon the surviving charter members began to grumble about the goal. Rally day arrived and, much to the dismay of the charter folks, the attendance exceeded the goal by 15. One of the "saints" stopped the elated pastor in the foyer and asked with a stoic expression, "Well, preacher, ya got your 200 here. Now whatcha gonna do with 'em?"

"It was a valid question," he said later. "What was my plan for assimilating them into the fellowship of the church? How would I guide them from the celebration in the sanctuary to the relationships in the Sunday School classroom?"

They were questions that would greatly influence his entire ministry. The questions served as a reminder to him that "body life" is more important than "body counts."

Steve Fortosis is quoted in the book *Is There a Future for the Sunday School?* as saying there are five important trends in today's Sunday School: "(1) new members participate more than regular members; (2) women and older adults have a more positive attitude toward Sunday School than younger adults and men; (3) how Sunday School influences the Christian growth of attendees is the most important variable; (4) fellowship is the prime motivation for adult involvement; and (5) the number of years of church membership has little if any influence on an adult's attitude toward Sunday School."

The goal of the Sunday School is to move from counting people to making people count! In his *Christianity Today* article "How Many Did You Have Last Sunday?" Jack Hayford confessed, "I played the numbers game. I lived in the shadow of three-digit attendance figures. I thought the day I broke 100 a peace would fill my soul. When it happened, solace was temporary, and soon I was haunted again. Only the numbers had changed." Hayford says he believes in "counting sheep" but also warned about being more concerned with numbers than God's blessing. He adds that each church has an integral strength, and some seem to experience greater growth. "One church may be characterized by its evangelism program, another by its teaching ministry, others by their emphases on miracles, missions, small groups, prayer, etc. God is not indicating their superiority or His preference by granting growth. He's simply directing our attention to things that are important to Him. . . . The challenge for me is to listen to the Holy Spirit and to quit measuring my pastoral success by playing the numbers game."[2]

C. Peter Wagner makes the analogy between the physical body and the Body of Christ, the Church. He says there are certain vital signs that indicate health, one of which is meeting member needs. "To be attractive to newcomers, a church has to serve its members well. If it does, it will produce satisfied customers, so to speak, who will in turn spread the news that the church is doing things that appeal to outsiders as well."[3]

"Gone are the days when attendance taking was
so subtle that you wondered how they did it."

Serving our "customers" well includes assimilating
them into the very life of the church. And Sunday School
is an important entry point for that assimilation. Dr. Gary
McIntosh, in his *Church Growth Network Newsletter,*
says, "Involvement in genuine friendships, participation in
small-group fellowship, and a sense of community help
create a bond with the congregation. The sense of 'belong-
ing' is imperative in assimilating new people into the life
of a congregation."[4]

"Welcome to Wal-Mart!"

The image of the smiling face and the offered shopping cart at the discount store chain is all too familiar. The
"Wal-Mart" welcome has since been emulated by almost
every organization. That famous "Welcome!" has become
synonymous with the store and its philosophy of customer

service. Adults of different ages, socioeconomic background, work experience, and even physiological strengths have been pressed into service—but not without training in the fine art of "welcoming."

Some churches have learned the art of welcoming people and have seen growth both in numbers and in body life as a result. Other churches are on the south end of the learning curve. They have a lot of visitors, but those visitors don't come back. Many people who come through our church doors are like Jenni. She relates her experience:

> A couple I know invited me to church. I got there early and sat in a pew about midway. I looked up when people walked by, hoping someone would stop and talk to me. The pews around me filled, but no one said a word. If someone had only looked at me, I could have probably started the conversation.

> After church, I took my time picking up my purse and Bible and walking toward the door. But again, no one spoke. My friends weren't there, so I left feeling embarrassed and awkward and not wanted.

The story has a happy ending because Jenni kept trying and eventually found her niche. But what about the people who aren't persistent or who don't know how to make friendship moves? We can alleviate much of the "back door exodus" by developing friendliness in our churches—starting with our leaders. There are some important steps in creating a "Wal-Mart" welcome in your Sunday School or church.

1. Station informed greeters at all doors.

Greeters make visitors feel at home and help them know where to go, but the greeter's job includes more. Greeters set the tone for the whole church. If they are friendly and accommodating, it breaks the ice for all church members. Greeters should be stationed at *all* doors. Some churches even station them in the parking lot.

Don't let just anyone be a greeter. Choose and train

people who are not shy, but can initiate conversation. Greeters and ushers are some of the most important "public relations" people in your church.

2. Strategize welcoming gestures.

One or more persons can be assigned the task of watching for visitors and sending other members to greet new people. Most people would be more than happy to be on the "Hello! Committee" to make someone feel welcomed—they just need to be asked or reminded to do so.

3. Clarify procedures.

Regular attendees and members may know to refer to the bulletin for special choruses or corporate scripture reading. However, when you don't direct visitors where to look or what to do, they may feel out of place. Some churches have "pew captains" who are responsible for making guests in their pew feel welcomed and informed about the service. In a tactful way, they make sure the visitor gets to know other people in their pew, has a bulletin, visitor card, hymnal, pew Bible, and so forth.

4. Teach your leaders basic principles on how to start and maintain a conversation.

What are the basic principles? In a nutshell:

a. Make the first move. Say "Hello!"

b. Ask guests general questions. Do they live nearby? Have they ever attended this church before? What kind of activities do they like?

c. Keep the focus on the other person, not yourself. Keep the conversation moving and interesting to him or her. Avoid controversial topics.

d. Offer explanations. Tell guests who people are. Fill them in on what the class or pastor has been discussing. Talk about the activities offered by the church.

e. Introduce the guest to others. But don't leave him or her at their mercy. Help the visitor find common conversational ground with others.

5. Give guests written material.

All churches should have brochures, which include basic information about the services of the church, its basic beliefs, its statement of purpose, and its programs (include contact people, telephone numbers, and days and times of activities). Visitors may forget or not fully understand if it's not in writing.

6. Invite guests to the next service.

"Will we see you tonight? In fact, why don't you sit with us?" To a visitor who truly wants to find a church home, those are welcomed words.

7. Learn to remember names.

Write the visitors' names down later. Use their names when introducing them to others. And, try your best to remember the visitors' names the next time you see them.

8. Invite guests to classes, small groups, or social functions.

Get the names of visitors to those who have the gift of hospitality. Sometimes we draw back from taking care of visitors because we're afraid of being too pushy. But it's probably best to err on the side of being too zealous than not being zealous enough in welcoming new people.

People are looking for a friendly, caring church. Make sure your church is a place where seekers find a genuine fellowship.

Cutting-edge Sunday Schools pay attention to the needs of people. They notice such things as an attendee who doesn't seem to act as cheerful. They are concerned about absentees. They notice when people skip their normal attendance routines. They are people-focused. Why? God loves people.

Jesus died for people.

Heaven and hell are inhabited by people.

Keeping It Personal in a Digital Age

It's entirely possible to spend several hours on the telephone these days and never speak to a human voice. Computer-generated voices impersonally answer our questions or refer us to another number on the telephone Touch-Tone pad. Weather alerts are even advised by a machine.

Sunday Schools have the opportunity to provide a human touch. Leaders, teachers, and workers can truly "reach out and touch" people starving for personal attention. They can add the personal to the digital. A telephone call can follow-up an E-mail message. A brief visit can supplement an advertising campaign.

Every effort can and must be made to be the eyes, the hands, and the feet of the Master. According to George W. Bullard, quoted in *Net Results,* "At least 2.5 billion persons (representing some 16,750 distinct societies, speaking more than 5,200 distinct languages or dialects) have no indigenous church, no cultural near-neighbors from whom they are likely to be exposed to an indigenized (and therefore understandable) expression of faith."[5]

I do not like to see the pastor on Sunday morning running around trying to find substitute teachers or passing out roll books. The pastor provides vision and leadership for the Sunday School. The pastor cannot give better shepherd care to the whole flock than through Sunday School.
—Elmer Towns

The Church must get another glimpse of the Savior on the hillside, "O Jerusalem, Jerusalem, you who kill the prophets and stone those sent to you, how often I have longed to gather your children together, as a hen gathers her chicks under her wings, but you were not willing" (Matt. 23:37). Today's Church must hear the heartbeat of the One who was people-focused and purpose-driven in all of His earthly ministry.

REDISCOVERY ACTION STEP
Providing Pastoral Care in Your Sunday School

- Compile a care list of six to eight students, listing names, addresses, phone numbers, and other pertinent information.

- Review your list daily and pray for the spiritual, emotional, financial, and relational needs.

- Build relationships with them, getting to know them by first and last name. Be able to identify care list members by name if you were to see them downtown or run into them at a store. Learn about their family—how many children they have, names, ages, and so forth. In short, be their friend.

- Look for them each Sunday. Watch for your care list friends as you enter Sunday School or church each week. Call them within 24 hours if they are absent, and let them know they were missed.

- Use a note or telephone call to express your continuing concern.

- As much as possible, try to meet needs you observe in their lives.

- Periodically, use some tangible gift (e.g., baked goods) as an expression of your friendship and concern for people on your care list.

- Be a source of encouragement and support.

- Watch for spiritual backsliding and lovingly warn them (without being judgmental).

- Provide resource materials for their spiritual growth (books, magazines, etc.).

Rediscovering Promotion in the Sunday School

The disciples went out and preached everywhere,
and the Lord worked with them and confirmed
his word by the signs that accompanied it.
(Mark 16:20)

THE PASTOR WAS PREOCCUPIED with thoughts of how he was going to ask the congregation to come up with more money than they were expecting for repairs to the church building. Upon his arrival at church on Sunday morning, he was annoyed to learn the regular organist was sick and a substitute had been brought in at the last minute. The substitute organist inquired about what to play for the worship service.

"Here's a copy of the service," responded the pastor. "But you'll have to think of something to play after I make the announcement about church finances."

At the appropriate time in the service, the pastor paused and said, "Brothers and sisters, we are in great difficulty; the roof repairs cost twice as much as we expected, and we need $4,000 more. I want everyone who will pledge at least $100 to please stand up."

Being a quick thinker, the substitute organist played "The Star-spangled Banner." And everyone stood!

Knowing how to promote the Sunday School is as difficult as knowing how to raise dollars for church ministries. Not every church has a "promoter" like the substitute church organist.

Why Sunday School? The response to this question too many times has been a puzzled look or a faraway glance, as though we are remembering better days. Now, thanks to the soul-searching investigation of people in the trenches and on the front lines, the answer to this question is crystal clear, ringing with truth born out of experience.

Dr. David M. Vaughn, a pastor in Lawrenceville, Georgia, responds:

I believe in Sunday School because it was there that I learned my basic theology.

I believe in Sunday School because it introduced me to a lifelong love for the Word of God.

I believe in Sunday School because it became my first accountability group.

I believe in Sunday School because it was there that I received my first ministry assignment.

I believe in Sunday School because I found a fellowship that I desperately needed as a new Christian.

Does that sound like a commercial for Sunday School? Yes! Unashamedly, yes! When you find something that works, the obvious response is to tell others about it.

On the Grow Again

The sign in front of the new McDonald's restaurant put form and substance to the growth strategy of the parent company: "On the Grow Again." They say what can and should be said of the outreach evangelism passion of Sunday School and related ministries. In fact, in looking back to the life and ministry of the Church described in the Book of Acts, the words come alive. "The word of God continued to increase and spread" (Acts 12:24). Again, "The word of the Lord spread widely and grew in power" (19:20). The first-century Church personified the common expression "Spread the word!" Because of the diligence in spreading the word about Christ's victory over the grave and of the fellowship of the Christ-ones, "The Lord added to their number daily" (2:47).

When people have a vision to grow, growth can occur, even in the midst of an unbelieving world. The 1st-century Church manifested a joyful acceptance of Christ and His Word, a commitment to sound doctrine, and recognition of fellowship in small groups. This Church was also characterized by dependency on prayer, a common faith, and a unity of passion and purpose.

The results were clear and measurable. Three thousand souls were added, and again, "the word of God grew and multiplied."

Sunday School leaders and workers can experience the same great fulfillment in the life of the Church in the 21st century as the Early Church discovered in the 1st century.

If a fast-food chain can enthusiastically strategize to market its product, certainly the Church can recapture its sense of mission to touch a world for Christ with its focus on people and the powerful Word of God. It can be "On the Grow Again!"

The ministry of education truly ministers when it is committed to the task of bringing people to Christ, building them up in Christ, and sending them out for Christ.

—Paul L. Walker

Sunday School Growth Factors

What are the primary ingredients in Sunday School growth?

Sunday Schools that grow have:

1. *A definite purpose.* Sunday Schools usually grow on purpose. There is a time in the life of a growing local church

when its leaders make a unified decision to put growth principles to work. For some, it would be easier to relax in the last part of Paul's account, "I planted the seed, Apollos watered it, but God made it grow" (1 Cor. 3:6). Granted, God does cause growth—He seems to place His blessings on certain ministries. His providential will allows spiritual rain to fall on some spiritual soil and an unusual harvest results—seemingly in a supernatural and spontaneous manner.

It's the same in Sunday School ministries. Growth is a by-product of God's blessing and our cooperative (and purposeful) efforts. Several definitive actions by those who labor with God must be included if there is to be a harvest and growth:

- Reaching—a plan to numerically expand the borders of ministry

- Teaching—a plan to effectively transfer the truths of God's Word

- Winning—a plan to present the claims of Christ to unbelievers

- Discipling—a plan to instruct new Christians in following Christ

- Training—a plan to disciple new Christians for ministry in the church

2. *A personal commitment to spiritual growth.* Growing and maturing Sunday Schools are led by growing and maturing Christians. Jesus said, "A good tree cannot bear bad fruit, and a bad tree cannot bear good fruit" (Matt. 7:18). Promotion without emotion is merely a "resounding gong or a clanging cymbal" according to Paul's word to Christians in Corinth (1 Cor. 13:1). Effective ministry comes from the heart—not just the head. Plans without power result in only temporary results. A growing and maturing Sunday School leader takes advantage of spiritual growth resources:

- Prayer and Bible study

- Devotional and ministry books

- Counsel of mature Christians
- Audio and video training tapes
- On-line resources

3. *A specific plan for growth.* Jesus called for sanctified strategy, "Suppose one of you wants to build a tower. Will he not first sit down and estimate the cost to see if he has enough money to complete it?" (Luke 14:28). Whether you're building a tower or a Sunday School, careful evaluation and planning are certainly in order. What definite steps ("cost") are you willing to take over the next several months or years?

Pastor Keith Grove of the Southwest Church of the Nazarene in Indianapolis, Indiana, plans for Sunday School growth every fall and spring. Study his action plan below for his spring campaign:

Spring Sunday School Campaign
Easter Sunday, April 4—Pentecost Sunday, May 23
Contacts + Consistency = Sunday School & Worship Growth

Pastor Keith	25 per week = 200
Pastor Baker	25 per week = 200
Pastor Perry	25 per week = 200
Sunday School Superintendent	10 per week = 80
Evangelism Committee Chairman	10 per week = 80
Teachers (12+Tary+Marlo & Kim=15) (5 each)	75 per week = 600
Students/Helpers	80 per week = <u>640</u>
	2,000

What is a contact? Phone call, visit, invitation, card, letter, flyer, doorknob hanger, any type of contact to invite to Sunday School/church, to offer encouragement or counsel. Just make contacts with people and share the love of Jesus and turn in each week.

Note the Numerical Progress of Our Campaign

	Total	Grand Total	S.S. Attendance	A.M. Worship
April 4	250	250	136	238
April 11	253	503	148	180
April 18	220	723	169	206
April 25	291	1,014	161	195

- Cooperate with the denomination's Sunday School growth emphasis.
- Launch a Sunday School class and schedule reorganization.
- Plan a facility's renovation or implement a building program.
- Add a second Sunday School session.
- Develop an off-campus Sunday School.
- Reach a new cultural group.

4. *A promotional campaign.* Based on a biblical theme, and with an evangelistic goal in mind, churches with growing Sunday Schools are keenly aware of "marketing" their "product." The "end" of their campaign is always the winning of souls and the discipling of Christians, but their "means to an end" are varied and will motivate and cause excitement. Their emphases may include a spring and fall themed campaign, or it may be a special thrust on one or more of the natural "high days" in the church year:

- Christmas
- Easter
- Pentecost Sunday
- Mother's Day
- Father's Day
- Independence Day or Canada Day Celebration

Sunday School promotion Sundays may also include:
- Baby dedication Sunday
- Friend Day
- Senior citizens Sunday
- Public safety worker recognition
- Teacher appreciation

Whatever the emphasis, the local Sunday School may be assured of several things:
1. Promotional campaigns attract new people.

2. Promotional campaigns motivate people to work.
3. Promotional campaigns utilize the skills of church members.
4. Promotional campaigns publicize the church's ministry.
5. Promotional campaigns are a commitment to work.

Marketing 101

There is nothing inherently spiritual about a marketing plan—and there is nothing inherently unspiritual about it. Marketplace tools can be utilized in the ministry. Secular techniques can be turned to sacred purposes.

The new technology led to greater efficiency at First Church.

We must resist the notion that "marketing" is only for toothpaste and condominiums if we love the church and want others to know about it. Congregations need to be skilled in marketing their churches. A philosophy for marketing (promoting) the Sunday School is found in author Stan Toler's book *The People Principle, Transforming Laypersons into Leaders.* Consider these elements:

Product. In the church the product is relationships. The consumer world talks about its product at every opportunity. In the church each person is in the business of building relationships. Can you say about your church, "You can find a friend in this fellowship"?

Price. Advertisers convince us that the price doesn't matter when you consider the product. Our price in the church is commitment. "When you join our church, you are going to have to get involved. It is going to take time and effort from you. We are not going to give you free parking passes and privileges. In fact, we may even ask you to park in the lot next door in order to make room for new people."

Place. Realtors say the three most important words in business are location, location, location. For the Church, the word "place" means "presence of believers." Each church is unique because of the mixture of its members. You can say, "There is no church like this church anywhere near this church." Acts 4:31 says, "After they prayed, the place where they were meeting was shaken." Your place can shake.

Promotion. Let people know the Good News. What are you doing to increase the flow of guests into your church? Do you introduce yourself, invite them to be a part of the family of God? Just as you prepare your home for guests coming for dinner, you need to prepare your church with the same anticipation. Treat guests as special people. Make sure your property is kept clean, painted, and well marked.

Can people find you in the yellow pages or find your driveway from the road? Do you promote your church on radio spots or through press releases and ads in your local newspapers? Develop attractive pamphlets and brochures to distribute in the community or by mail for your special programs or campaigns. Offer night classes for the community on single life, computer literacy, making the Bible user-friendly, or building your marriage. If you have a great place, make sure that the right people know about it.[1]

The Elements of Successful Marketing

Public relations differs from marketing in that public relations means telling the story to benefit your concerns, whereas marketing means appealing to the needs, interests, desires, and goals of others. Marketing includes telling them how their goals can be reached by linking with your specific resources. This is at the heart of successful marketing campaigns.

Simply, marketing techniques include several main ingredients:

1. *It must focus on meeting needs.*

Marketing begins with a commitment to meet the needs of your potential audience. It includes analysis, forecasting, and production, but in the ministry of the church, its end result is meeting spiritual, emotional, and social needs. It envisions programs and services, to which that target audience could respond. The emphasis here is on the term "could respond." That means variety, scheduling, and availability are issues to be considered when developing ministries, programs, and services.

2. *It must be targeted to a specific audience.*

You have no doubt received brochures or flyers through the mail advertising the start-up of a new church. If you have noticed, most suggest an array of services or ministries—front-door evangelism or side-door evangelism efforts—that appeal to the interests and needs of a specific people-group. The start-up organization may have chosen their target group by establishing a "focus group" (a sample of the population that represent the targeted audience) in that community and making inquiry of the group about what their "church needs" might be. Promotional and programming ideas can be derived from their ideas. Their reaction may also help to gauge the possible success of the program—and help in its development. Marketing is always focused.

3. *The target audience must be fully understood.*

Sunday School teacher Jim Marshall was lecturing on the subject of perseverance—"He drove straight to his goal. He looked neither to the right, nor to the left, but pressed forward, moved by a definite purpose. Neither friend nor foe could delay him nor turn him from his course. All who crossed his path did so at their own peril. What would you call such a man?"

Little Seth responded quickly, "A truck driver!"

Church leadership must not be confused about the target audience they are trying to reach. There must be a clear understanding of the demographic group to which you are targeting your resources and your program. Not understanding the target audience may indeed cause the church to offer an array of services and resources that simply are out of tune or out of touch with the needs of the target audience. It is essential to explore all of the ramifications of the target audience before making any kind of promotional effort.

Until this is done, more research is needed. Every large corporation fully researches the target audience to whom it will be marketing and endeavors to appeal to those perspectives unique to that audience, recognizable to that audience, and most likely to generate a favorable response.

4. *It must focus on reaching the responsibility list (Sunday School enrollment).*

Pastor Mike Williams, who serves as chairman of the Sunday School Ministries Convention for the North Central Ohio District Church of the Nazarene, recently built an entire convention around the theme: Taking Responsibility for the Responsibility List. Mike delineated the convention as follows:

Purpose: To encourage each church present to commit to a year-long process of "taking responsibility for the responsibility list."

Mike, along with other seminar leaders, focused on principles to promote the responsibility list.

Principles to Promote: To take responsibility for the responsibility list means . . .

1. You must have a church that is committed to taking responsibility for the responsibility list.

2. You must have an accurate responsibility list that includes an active responsibility list, a prospect list, and an extended list.

3. You must have classes or groups that operate from a perspective of spiritual gifts.

4. You must have classes or groups structured to give priority to providing "care ministries" for those on their responsibility list.

5. You must have classes or groups that plan regular events or activities that bind people together.

6. You must have classes or groups whose lessons lead people to the place of full salvation.

—Mike Williams
North Central Ohio District
Church of the Nazarene

Growing a Zero-Based Sunday School

With a rising median age, it is entirely possible to see churches without child attendees. Herb Miller in a *Net Results* article, "Reinventing the Sunday School in Childless Churches," offered a six-month plan to grow a zero-based Sunday School. Noting "the only way to grow a zero-based Sunday school is through a 'big bang' procedure in which four classes containing several children start simultaneously," he offered the following steps:

Step 1 (March): Present the growth plan to your church leaders, reminding them of the effort that it will take to reinvent the Sunday School.

Step 2 (April): Begin unfolding the plan to the congregation. Remind the parishioners that there is no early retirement from ministry, and the teaching skills of congregational members will be needed. Outline the four classes (preschool, grades one and two, grades three and four, and grades five and six). Call for a team of teachers and assistants, asking congregational members to prayerfully consider their part in the plan.

Step 3 (May): Recruit the eight-person teacher team. Meet with the teaching team, and outline the purpose and the plan for reinventing the Sunday School.

Step 4 (May—1st week): Ask the congregation to help develop a potential list of Sunday School students. Before the end of June, you should have a list of over 100 potential students in order to reach a goal of six enrollees in each of the four fall classes.

Step 5 (May—3rd week): Using commitment cards, ask the Sunday morning congregation to commit to praying daily for a goal of 24 children in Sunday School the first Sunday after Labor Day.

Step 6 (early July): Mail a letter from the superintendent to all prospects. Address the parents and advise them that, with their permission, you would like to have their child (use the child's name) attend a newly organized Sunday School. Also, advise them that someone will be contacting them later in the summer to verify their permission for the child to attend.

Step 7 (last 2 weeks of July): Organize members of the congregation to visit the homes of potential students (assigning visitors to people they know if possible). Visitors would remind parents of potential students of the organizing Sunday School for their child's (name) age and ask permission to invite the child. (Possible visitation schedule: 2 weeks, 4-7:30 P.M. visitation, 8 P.M. dessert and sharing time.)

Step 8 (3rd week of August): Have congregation members mail invitation letters (using model letter) to potential students whose parents have given you permission to contact. (Ask members who know the potential students to write the letter if possible.)

Step 9 (4th week of August): The pastor sends a personal letter to the potential students, introducing the teachers and reminding them of the Sunday School's beginning date.

Step 10 (Tuesday evening prior to beginning Sunday): Organize a telephone team to contact the potential students (between 6 and 8 P.M.). Remind them of the starting time, and ask parents if the children need transportation. Try to talk to the child first, and then to the parents. The telephone callers may meet at the church for coffee and a reporting session after the calling time.

Step 11 (Wednesday prior to the beginning Sunday): Pastor writes letters to potential students who have responded in a positive way. Remind the students of the class time and the name of their teacher, and advise the child that the pastor will welcome them upon their arrival.

Step 12: Celebrate the results in the morning worship service on the beginning Sunday. Meet with the teaching team in the afternoon to discuss class needs. Establish a system for handwriting notes to absentees on subsequent Sundays.

Miller adds, "Research of the Gallup organization and others indicates that more than three-fourths of unchurched adults would like to see their children involved in Christian education. This is a fertile field in which to sow seeds. Plant them with care and results will follow."[2]

- Submit announcements to your community paper.
- Post flyers on bulletin boards in grocery stores, child care centers, and so forth.
- Display yard signs.

- Send direct mail to new residents.
- Hold backyard Bible schools in surrounding neighborhoods.
- Conduct a telephone canvas.
- Enter a float in a community parade.
- Sponsor family life seminars.
- Announce classes on local TV community calendar.
- Write public service announcements for local radio stations.

REDISCOVERY ACTION STEP
Defining Your Ministry Community

1. Define your immediate ministry area.
   - Plot your church membership on a community map.
   - Determine distances you can expect people to travel.
   - Fix a geographical area using the expected travel distance.

2. Determine potential ministry groups.
   - Identify people groups in your community through local agencies.
   - Research and develop a ministry profile for each people group.

3. Profile your church membership.
   - Profile your church membership (name, age, education, interests, gifts).
   - Identify friends and relatives who are potential attendees through member referrals.

4. Implement one of the Sunday School campaigns located in the appendices.

Rediscovering the Sunday School Team

*The people were amazed at his teaching, because he taught them
as one who had authority, not as the teachers of the law.*
(Mark 1:22)

TWO MEN met on the street. One said to the other, "Have
you heard about John? He embezzled the company out of
a half a million dollars."

The other man said, "That's terrible; I never did trust
John."

The first man said, "Not only that, he left town and he
took Tom's wife with him."

The other man said, "That's awful; John has always
been a no-good."

The first man said, "Not only that, he stole a car to
make his getaway."

The other man said, "That's scandalous; I always did
think John had a bad streak in him."

The first man said, "Not only that, they think he was
drunk when he pulled out of town."

The other man said, "John's no good. But what really
bothers me is, who's going to teach his Sunday School
class this week?"

Staffing the Sunday School team with godly leaders
who live the holiness lifestyle is a challenging assignment.

The word "legacy" is a term used in the legal sense of

property in possessions, money, and other gifts being handed down or left to family or friends with someone's passing. Legacy is also more than a reference to things. It is, in a greater sense, what we are remembered for—and why.

In his second letter to Timothy, the apostle Paul wrote powerful words that give us guidelines for leaving a legacy through the Sunday School to generations yet to come: "Continue in what you have learned and have become convinced of, because you know those from whom you learned it" (3:14). The reference is clear—Timothy's teachers had left a legacy worth remembering.

Sunday School staffing is key to the spiritual and numerical growth of the local church. For instance, one of your first church memories is probably of a Sunday School teacher. In one of his last published articles, Randal Denny, a longtime friend of both of us, wrote:

Sunday School is more important than quarterlies and promotional gimmicks. The influence of committed godly men and women builds a powerful network in which to nurture Christians—new and experienced, young and old. Even down in our church's furnace room, my Sunday School teacher influenced me toward Jesus. Our pastor's wife, Mrs. Lyle Potter, was a classy lady with a twinkle of joy in her happy eyes. I still remember her in that dimly lit furnace room, with her pupils gathered around her, as a model of Christian womanhood. I can't remember a single lesson, but my whole life has been influenced by a gracious, caring lady with an infectious lilt of laughter who pointed to Jesus.

Your Sunday School is more important than you think! It may be avant-garde to diminish the place of Sunday School, but I suspect you have yet to find something better. Marion Lawrence said, "First I learned to love my teacher, then I learned to love my teacher's Bible, then I learned to love my teacher's Savior."[1]

Many Sunday School workers ask us, "How can I become a godly, caring, sucessful Sunday School teacher?" We believe the following 12 ingredients reflect successful Sunday School leadership.

How to Be a Successful Teacher

- Be personally committed to Christ and the church.
- Make Christianity vital, alive, and important.
- Show concern for those you teach.
- Handle discipline with love and concern for the student.
- Keep in touch with your class during the week.
- Make your classroom attractive so students know you care about them.
- Provide the opportunity to experience God in their midst.
- Develop a creative and meaningful classroom style.
- Be in class before the first student arrives.
- Don't just talk about Christianity; live it!
- Know the Bible.
- Plan to grow your class.

Teachers Worth Remembering

Consider the legacy of teachers worth remembering as outlined by Paul to Timothy, and let it be a pattern for your Sunday School staff.

1. Teachers worth remembering know the times.

It is imperative that teachers know the times. Along with a thorough knowledge of God's Word, teachers can make themselves aware of current events and current trends. Weaving a mention of something current into the lesson by way of illustration can be an effective communication link. Subscribing to a local newspaper or a newsmagazine may be well worth the investment if some reference or illustration drives home a scriptural truth to a student.

For example, a high school teacher doesn't have to listen to the same music his or her students are listening to, to know what's on the Top 40. Newspapers often list the top songs and the teacher can pick out a relevant title—or even find a source for the lyrics—and tie the song into a lesson or lesson illustration.

A current event could well be a great discussion starter in an adult class and provide a bridge into the scripture being studied that week. The mention of the current event speaks to the student not only of the teacher's awareness but also about the relevance of God's Word.

2. Teachers worth remembering know the pattern.

A life well lived is more important than a lesson well prepared. Every teacher who holds a Bible in his or her hand in front of a class should ask the Holy Spirit for help, not only in teaching the principles in that book but in living them as well.

Teachers worth remembering believe the Holy Spirit for personal cleansing and empowering to live exemplary lives before their students. Their victory over the attitudes and events of time is a great incentive to their students.

3. Teachers worth remembering know the students.

Carl George said, "Unless the pupil comes first, the lesson will never take root in the life." Students must know they are unequivocally accepted and loved.

It is interesting to read in Matt. 11 what was being said about John the Baptist and about Jesus, the Son of Man. The record says, "John came neither eating nor drinking, and they say, 'He has a demon.' The Son of Man came eating and drinking, and they say, 'Here is a glutton and a drunkard, a friend of tax collectors and "sinners"'" (vv. 18-19).

Jesus, a friend of sinners? It is true.

Friendship with sinners does not suggest friendship with sinfulness. It does, however, invite conscious, deliberate commitment to know more sinners and to love and lead more sinners to the greatest of all Lover of sinners, Jesus. In fact, it was His love for sinners that moved God to action, "Because of his great love for us, God, who is rich in mercy, made us alive with Christ even when were dead in transgressions" (Eph. 2:4-5).

Twenty-first century Sunday Schools will face moral issues unlike those of any previous age. Students will come to our classes with values totally unlike ours. We can fully reject those values that contradict Scripture, but we cannot reject the one who holds them. Teachers worth remembering have a spirit of loving acceptance.

4. Teachers worth remembering know the source of life.

In Sunday School we talk about "discovering the Word." It is more than a slogan; it is the source of life. Think about what Paul said, "All Scripture is God-breathed and is useful for teaching, rebuking, correcting and training in righteousness" (2 Tim. 3:16). Dr. William Lyon Phelps, one of Yale University's most distinguished professors, said, "I would rather have a thorough knowledge of the Scriptures than a college education." Phelps understood that God's Word is the great commentary on all other words. His knowledge of Scripture enhanced all of his learning.

Students don't expect their teachers to know every chapter, verse, and line of the Bible, but they expect their teachers to have a basic Bible knowledge. They expect their teacher to love God's Word—more than a commentary or quarterly. A teacher's time with the Word of God makes the time in the classroom more meaningful.

In a world of myriad philosophies, the single and most reliable source of truth—the Bible—must be the *main thing*. Teachers worth remembering will feed daily on the Bread of Life.

"Pay" Your Staff

Someone discovered some "Rules for Teachers," dated 1872, in a historic wooden schoolhouse. One of the

Actual Responses to Bible Questions
by Elementary Age Students

1. Moses went to the top of Mount Cyanide to get the Ten Commandments.
2. The seventh commandment is "Thou shalt not admit adultery."
3. Joshua led the Hebrews in the Battle of Geritol.
4. Jesus was born because Mary had an immaculate contraption.
5. The people who followed Jesus were called the 12 Decibels.
6. The epistles were the wives of the apostles.
7. One of the opossums was St. Matthew.
8. Paul preached acrimony, which is another name for marriage.

Ten Commandments for the Sunday School Worker

1. Thou shalt not hide from the leadership role to which God has called you and that the church has given you, nor shrink from spiritual help in the task of reaching out into the community and touching lives for the Lord Jesus Christ.
2. Thou shalt not neglect to set goals that will encourage growth in your Sunday School, not just for numbers but to reach individual souls for the Master.
3. Thou shalt not endeavor to do the task of leading your Sunday School alone but will encourage others to pray and to help obtain the goals you have set.
4. Thou shalt remember that the Sunday School is to magnify the Lord Jesus Christ and to edify the church and its members.

5. Thou shalt visit, enlist, encourage, and teach those in your class, helping them to grow in Christian love and attitudes.
6. Thou shalt not kill the enthusiasm of the Sunday School, for learning is fun when cheerfulness, concern, and love exist.
7. Thou shalt commit the Sunday School class into God's hands for nurture, love, and sharing His relationship through your teaching and reaching and caring.
8. Thou shalt not steal time from the study of the Scriptures by not arriving on time and with trivial small talk.
9. Thou shalt not bear false accusations against the church but hold it up as God's instrument to reach out, touch lives, and win souls in the community for the Lord Jesus Christ.
10. Thou shalt not covet but borrow, improve, and use ideas of others that will bring growth, learning, and enjoyment to the Sunday School classroom, so that in all that is done we will magnify the Lord.

—Jane Landreth

rules stated, "The teacher who performs his labor faithfully and without fault for 5 years will be given an increase of 25 cents per week in his pay, providing the Board of Education approves."

There has been an interesting discussion over the past several years. People are asking, "Should we pay Sunday School workers?"

The answer is, "Yes!"

We should "pay" them—not with a paycheck but with other "currency."

When we begin to pay them, they will be happier and better able to serve the Sunday School. Here are some appropriate ways to "pay" the hardworking staff members of your Sunday School.

1. Appreciation

Pastors and Sunday School leaders must show appreciation to staff members. A simple "Thank you" lifts the spirits and helps the attitudes of the workers. Like any other volunteers, Sunday School staff members need this verbal encouragement.

Something in a human's heart wants to know that he or she is appreciated for the things he or she does. When the need is not met, discouragement rushes in. Give your workers a "bonus," tell them how much you appreciate their efforts.

Thank-you notes and letters are also powerful ways of expressing gratitude. One Trinity Church of the Nazarene teacher responded to a simple thank-you card, "I was so moved when I read your card, I cried! I appreciate your sending it. I don't deserve it, but it surely felt good. Thanks."

2. Information

One of the best "paychecks" that leaders can give to their staff is good information about Sunday School plans and schedules. When leaders fail to communicate to staff members, the members get frustrated and stressed. They need to know what's going on in the Sunday School, and they can't be aware unless someone tells them.

Leaders should make phone calls or should publish changes in schedule, special student programs, training sessions, or anything else that affects the staff.

3. Training

Training is essential for all staff members, no matter how experienced they may be. Giving proper training is like paying your staff because the skills and methods they learn will continue to be valuable resources.

When the staff is properly trained, they do their jobs better and with less effort and frustration. They not only feel more confident but also enjoy their ministry more.

4. Incentives

Recognition feels good and it motivates staff members. Everybody likes to be recognized for their work. Pay your staff members with incentives and recognition, such as:

> Longevity awards—present plaques or other gifts to staff members who have served for 5, 10, or 15 years. Perseverance is difficult, and faithful commitment should be acknowledged.

> "Second Mile Award" recognition—Sunday Schools can use special awards to identify and recognize staff members who go the extra mile in their Sunday School ministry. The recognition may include inscribing their name on a plaque, a gift certificate, or a special reserved parking place.

Consider the Alternatives

Sunday School staffing in a day when the average mom spends the equivalent of 17 days per year transporting her children to school and recreational activities can be a real challenge. Leaders increasingly face empty classrooms and last-minute substitutions that diminish the quality of Christian education in the local church.

Quality education calls for qualified staff members who are highly motivated. Josh Hunt wrote, "The best recruiting starts with people and moves them toward ministry, not the other way around. We often start with the vacancy on the organizational chart and try to find someone to fill it. Jesus used a different approach. He started with the person and said, 'Go!'"[2]

Even highly motivated, ministry-driven workers experience burnout. Leaders must consider plan B when facing those empty spaces in the organizational chart. Some alternate staffing methods will still need to be considered.

- Team teaching
- Short-term assignments

- Assigning student interns
- Combined classes
- Video series

Your Sunday School ministries team will come up with some creative staffing ideas in a specially called brainstorming session.

The Weekly Leadership Seminar

One effective way to communicate with your Sunday School staff is to conduct a weekly leadership meeting. After an opening song and prayer, a brief report of the previous meeting may be given, the standard lesson may be reviewed, and teaching materials distributed. The weekly meeting is also a good time to recognize the efforts of the workers with some words of praise and a thank-you. The pastor or some other special speaker may close the meeting with a message that stirs the workers to give their best, and may outline the vision for the Sunday School.

Weekly leadership meetings will do the following:

- Help the workers gain a vision for the overall ministry.
- Affirm the importance of individual efforts.
- Improve communication.
- Provide a time of fellowship.
- Inspire workers to greater achievement.
- Give an opportunity for instruction.
- Encourage the spiritual growth of the worker.
- Promote outreach.
- Provide an opportunity to discuss and solve problems.
- Prepare the staff for their Sunday responsibilities.
- Allow a time for vision-casting.
- Alert workers to new attendees and members to be assimilated.
- Keep the workers stirred and challenged in their ministry.

Schedule a monthly Sunday
School leadership meeting. Be sure
to cover the four I's:
Information
Instruction
Involvement
Inspiration
—Stan Toler
101 Ways to Grow a Healthy Sunday School

Love Is the Key

At a pastors' gathering held at Southern Nazarene University, H. B. London told of returning to a place he once called home, Oklahoma City, to honor his grandfather, A. S. London, who was receiving an award from Southern Nazarene University. He reminisced about growing up in nearby Bethany with his cousin, James Dobson, learning to ride horses, and forging other lasting friendships. But most of all, he thought about the influence his grandfather had on his life.

Today, I read from the only book he ever wrote, titled *Love Is the Key*. He said, "Love touched the unclean leper and made him well again. It washed light into the eyes of the blind, and caused them to see. Love said to the 'scarlet woman,' 'Go in peace.' Love had compassion on the fainting multitudes and fed them in the wilderness. Love calls to every prodigal to come back to the father's house, and to every sinful Mary Magdalene to return to God for pardon and decency."

As I visit the site of "Pop's" burial, I will pause to thank him for loving me when I didn't deserve to be loved. "But the greatest of these is *love*" (1 Cor. 13:13, emphasis added).

REDISCOVERY ACTION STEP
Teaching Your Staff About
Class Discipline

Classroom discipline is one of the most unpleasant tasks facing the Sunday School worker. Discipline is what you make it. Approach it negatively and it becomes unpleasant. Be positive and the classroom experience can be rewarding. There are several steps to positive discipline:

- Establish rules and guidelines for the class.

- Let the class know what kind of behavior you expect.

- Try to be positive in your enforcement of rules—for example, don't say, "If you want to hear today's story, you will have to sit quietly."

- Be specific—good or bad behavior is too general for children. For instance, repeat your instructions to the class and take nothing for granted.

- Let each Sunday be a new day—tell yourself that the children will be good today. Attitude is half the battle. Always have a well-planned program for the class.

"Now for those wiggly kids in children's church . . . Velcro chairs!"

- Be consistent—if you say "No gum chewing" one Sunday, be sure you enforce the rule on the next Sunday as well. Never make a rule and then overlook it.
- Reward good behavior—if you reward good behavior, the class will work harder to improve. (Often bad behavior is attention-getting.)
- Showcase well-mannered and well-behaved pupils.
- Reinforce good class behavior.
- Praise students individually—and publicly.
- Develop class pride—"This is the best class in the Sunday School. I am proud of every one of you."

Rediscovering Multiple Sunday Schools

Then the church throughout Judea, Galilee and Samaria
enjoyed a time of peace. It was strengthened; and encouraged by
the Holy Spirit, it grew in numbers, living in the fear of the Lord.
(Acts 9:31)

IN A SMALL Oklahoma community, a Nazarene church was about to close. A Christian church pastor with a small congregation in the same town was conducting services without a permanent church building. Graciously, the small Nazarene group invited the Christian church group to meet in its building.

Ultimately, the Christian church pastor filled the pulpit for several years for both groups. The day came when they decided to merge the two congregations into one group. In a church business meeting, a decision centered on the possibility of a new church name. Some felt strongly that the name "Christian" should be used in the new name. An elderly gentleman stood and said, "I've been a Nazarene for 64 years, and you're not about to make a Christian out of me now!"

The story illustrates how difficult change can be for all of us. But an openness to change is the necessary ingredient in Sunday School growth.

Many ask, "Why do some of America's greatest churches seem to move in a great rhythmic flow—experiencing growth, winning and discipling new Christians, embracing a fresh vision for ministry?" Simply stated, many of those churches have rediscovered the powerful potential of Sunday School and they are willing to consider new methods.

The Sunday School is the Church organized for action because it is a people-focused agency and a purpose-driven movement. It still offers the local church the greatest potential for the crucial elements of local church ministry.

Again, those elements are:

• Reaching

• Teaching

• Winning

• Caring

Indeed, Sunday School is the one agency of the local church that is most in tune with the times.

• Sunday School promotes true community.

• Sunday School is truly intergenerational.

• Sunday School is cross-cultural.

• Sunday school possesses infinite potential for variety, customization, and location.

The new Sunday School is flexible and adaptable—so successful that many churches are looking for ways of multiplying this delivery system. One way is to unleash the power of multiple Sunday Schools.

The Multiple Sunday School

How do you add ministry without adding facilities? How do you naturally enlist additional workers in the Sunday School ministry? How do you double your potential for growth within your present congregation? The answers to these important questions may well be in adding *multiple Sunday School sessions*. Without doubt, multiple Sunday Schools have significantly helped many churches achieve their goals of outreach, evangelism, service, community-building, and nurture. Adding another Sunday School session is a logical, scriptural, and cost-effective way to expand your ministry base and reach out to unchurched people in your community. Interested? Here's how!

Begin with a Philosophy of Christian Education

Few, if any, churches choose to implement multiple Sunday Schools on the basis of a whim. Clearly, solid research and evaluation should precede any decision to implement an additional Sunday School session. Involve the whole leadership team in a Sunday School needs assessment. But don't overlook the fact that needs assessments can be performed by persons who have a myopic view of the ministry, rather than a global view. It is absolutely essential to make sure that all of the representative elements in your faith community have a significant level of buy-in.

Development of a time line for achieving selected sequences is important. Time lines are essential to helping an organization not only track its own performance but also monitor its well-being and its efficiency in using its resources.

A written planning guide accompanied by a checklist of tactical steps would also be very helpful. Of course, that guide will be tailored to fit your local church. While there will be many similarities and comparisons drawn between your ministry and other ministries, in reality you will face certain strategic differences that need to be incorporated in advance.

Another helpful place to begin is with your church's philosophy of Christian education. The story is told of the family who decided to leave the city and move to the country. They bought a ranch and made plans to raise cattle. About six months after completing the relocation process and the building of their ranch, some friends came to see them, wanting also to see the ranch and the cattle. The friend said to the owner of the ranch, "What do you call the ranch?"

The owner of the ranch said, "Well, that's a long story. I wanted to call it the Flying W, my wife wanted to name it the Suzie Q, my oldest son wanted to call it the Bar J, and my youngest son wanted to call it the Lazy Y.

His visitor replied, "So, what did you end up calling it?"

The rancher said, "We called it the Flying W, Suzie Q, Bar J, Lazy Y Ranch.

"That's quite a name," the friend said, "but where's the cattle?"

The owner sadly replied, "Well, we don't have any. You see, none of them survived the branding!"[1]

Church leaders face the same kinds of problems when they try to create a Christian education philosophy with a "one size fits all" brand. A focused philosophy of Christian education is just as essential as a philosophy of evangelism, compassionate ministries, discipleship, worship, or preaching ministry. Before you can implement a multiple Sunday School ministry, you must first develop a philosophy that defines what you are, what you want to be, and what you want to do. A people-focused, purpose-driven philosophy of Christian education is essential in undergirding any plans for additional Sunday School sessions. Some of the components of that philosophy will include the following:

1. A qualified leadership team

What qualifications does your church have regarding Sunday School staff selection? Are there certain standards that must be met before those individuals may participate as a teacher or worker? If so, do you wish to maintain those standards or are they up for review?

In what way does your current Sunday School leadership check for grace-giftedness on the part of Sunday School workers? Is this done through a recruiting practice? Are there formalized means of determining spiritual gifts and graces in the lives of the individuals that are currently involved in your Sunday School ministry?

2. A standard for lifestyle

Identifying personnel that are fully in agreement with your prevailing philosophy of Christian education prevents the square peg in a round hole syndrome. It is essential that individuals who are involved with your ministry are aligned with its philosophy.

A TV advertisement shows two mechanics leaning under the hood of an automobile attempting to replace a battery. The larger of the two mechanics is busy pounding away with a hammer trying to force the new part in the car while the other mechanic looks on approvingly. The owner of the car repeatedly questions the mechanics about the need for pounding on the part. His questions are legitimate. "Are you sure that's the right part? If so, why must you pound on it to make it fit?"

In the commercial, the respondents reply, "We'll make it fit! It will work!" And the ad does a "dream warp" showing a step back in time to where the two individuals appear to be young brothers playing on the floor of the family home. The older or larger one is pounding a square peg into a round hole of a child's toy. As the scene progresses, the peg, now in splinters and shattered, rests precariously in the hole while the younger of the two says to the larger or older child, "Good job! You made it fit!"[2]

3. The training of leaders

Sunday School leaders who are imbued with the core elements of your philosophy of Christian education need to be developed. They must not be individuals whose "square peg" philosophies need to be pounded into the structure of your ministry. Generally, it is through preaching, teaching, training, coaching, and mentoring that such Christian leaders are raised up. Pastors must reflect their philosophy of Christian education unique to your congregation in their preaching. The task of other leaders and trainers is to share the core values in order that staff may become not only informed of them but also captivated by them. Teachers must model that philosophy in teaching so that it will be caught by the students. Leaders are the pacesetters. They are responsible for reengineering, reinventing, or rebuilding the Sunday School.

In considering a move to multiple session Sunday Schools, that leadership, borne out of allegiance to the core values of the ministry, will affect your decisions. Does the desire to move to multiple sessions indicate an interest in reengineering the Sunday School to more effectively utilize the resources—including space, schedules, personnel, and so on? Or are you reinventing Sunday School—making an effort to raise up a Sunday School emphasis that has been in serious decline? Or are you simply rebuilding your Sunday School, endeavoring to take back ground that has been lost, to make up for time that has been wasted, or to strive to lift the level of performance?

Any of these three reasons are good reasons. However, if you are going to consider a move to multiple Sunday School sessions, and want to make sure that this desire is aligned with the core elements of your philosophy, make sure you have considered some relevant questions.

1. Shall we reeducate our current staff, or should we recruit and train new workers?

2. What priorities of time will we expect of the staff?

3. How will the ministry commitment be defined?

Asking the Right Questions

Part of the genius of leadership is asking the right questions. There are some specific questions the local church leaders should ask in considering multiple Sunday Schools:

1. Is there a real need for multiple Sunday Schools? Dr. Elmer Towns's 80 percent rule of functional space is true, whether it is related to worship services or Sunday School classroom space. For example, Dr. Towns says that architects estimate 18 inches per person are required to

adequately seat them in one location. In reality, people prefer not to touch each other whether they are seated in a classroom on individual chairs or in the sanctuary seated in a pew.

Lecterns, display tables, resource tables, and so forth, in Sunday School classrooms take up space that could be used for seating. Thus, in most Sunday Schools, many seats are not used simply because they restrict participation or vision.

Again according to Towns, approximately 25 percent of the members of a typical church are absent every Sunday morning. This means that only 75 percent of the members of a typical church are present in Sunday morning worship. Therefore, there are automatically capacity limitations for housing new Sunday School attendees.

2. Has the research been done? Have the key church leaders done adequate studies to determine whether a multiple Sunday School is a viable option?

- What are the age demographics?
- How will the facilities be affected?
- Will there be adequate staff?
- Will the budget allow for additional teaching resources?

3. What strategic barriers will be faced? Every new project faces certain barriers. In a positive sense, Dr. Bill Sullivan, at the 1997 TEACH Conferences said, "Churches reach a point in their history when something extraordinary is required in order to break through the barriers and achieve growth. On the other hand, every church leader knows there are some negative barriers that must also be overcome—whether they are real or imagined. Some of the barriers are related to buildings and facilities. Some are related to finance. Some are related to personnel. And others are related to longstanding traditions."

4. How will the idea of multiple Sunday Schools be "sold" to the congregation? While many may dislike the

use of marketing language in the context of the church, the reality is clear. "Shared ownership" is needed in the pursuit of a vision of this size. It would be difficult, if not impossible, to pursue adding an additional Sunday School without the support of the church's formal and informal leadership. They need to feel their input is desired and valued.

When we think about selling an idea, we must also overcome what many have called the classic seven last words of the church, "We've never done it that way before." Longstanding traditions and habits in the church are indeed difficult to overcome.

Much time must be spent in prayer and consensus-building in order to ensure that the vision is not just owned by only a small group. Rather, it must be a vision with the participation and ownership of the majority of the congregation.

5. Is there any "history" that will affect it? Often, when pastoral changes occur, memories and allegiance relating to past leadership tend to interfere with new ministry ideas and changes proposed by the current leader. A review of the past may reveal strategies that have been tried but subsequently failed.

Engaging a new ministry, including the multiple Sunday School model, in a local congregation clearly requires a review of the church's history. Any pastor or church leader that ignores this warning is certainly asking for difficulty in the days ahead.

6. What are the expectations, goals, and objectives? Such expectations, goals, and objectives must be clearly stated so that there is widespread congregational ownership. They should clearly reflect the church's mission in ways that enable the people to see the relationship of mission, values, tradition, and a vision for a growing Sunday School.

The Sunday School "Preliminaries"

Back when Sunday Schools had "opening exercises" that included singing, birthday offerings, visitor recognition, and attendance reports, those exercises were referred to as "the preliminaries." The preliminaries often set the tone for the entire Sunday School hour.

Preliminaries are observed in other endeavors also. Consider air travel, for example. Thankfully, most commercial airlines use flight manuals and a preliminary flight checklist. The reason is threefold: (1) to ensure accurate step-by-step directions for successfully carrying out the flight plan; (2) to ensure the safety of all passengers; and, (3) to complete their assignment in a financially prudent manner. Those flight manuals are as essential as the preflight training sessions whether you are NASA planning a trip to the moon or United Airlines planning a trip to Miami.

Similarly, without a step-by-step checklist of the preliminaries, it is unlikely that any church moving to multiple Sunday School sessions will maximize the potential.

Implementing Multiple Sunday School Sessions

An automobile may be carefully designed. It might have all the right (and tested) parts in place. But if it is to be a viable mode of transportation, it must "take to the road." It's the same in multiple Sunday School ministries. There is a prayerfully and carefully considered moment when the plan is put into action. Several things will then happen:

- Staff will be recruited.
- Training sessions will be scheduled.
- Space allocation and scheduling will be planned.
- Information will be provided to the congregation and to the community.
- Direct mailing or telemarketing strategies will be used.

Program or Passion?

Simply adding another program module without an accompanying passion will result in burnout and division. The leadership has a decision to make that goes to the core of its existence. What will it be—symbols, mere reflections, and neat new programs? Or will the leaders in the church move forward and stake their promised claims on substance, renewal, and passion?

Leaders hold the keys that unlock the doors of unlimited opportunity for spiritual breakthrough and effective soul winning. It has often been repeated that "without Him we cannot and without us He will not." The church must move beyond symbols, reflection, and program to vitality through substance, renewal, and passion.

Multiple Sunday School sessions are not implemented to add another mark to the printed calendar or to carve another notch in the statistical belt of the church. They are implemented to reach men, women, boys, and girls with an anointed presentation of the gospel of Jesus Christ. If that is the supreme passion, then every effort it takes to make it happen has a glorious and an eternal significance.

REDISCOVERY ACTION STEP
A Checklist for Welcoming Sunday School Guests

Are well-trained, friendly, informed, and committed greeters in place?

Have the ushers been trained to make guests feel "at home"?

Is there an attractive, uncluttered, well-staffed Welcome Center?

Have the facilities been thoroughly cleaned and straightened?

Are the classrooms and worship areas clearly marked with attractive and informative signs?

Has the Sunday School staff been trained in welcoming guests?

Are there appropriate materials for guest registration?

Has the Sunday School lesson been well prepared?

Are there extra Bibles and other classroom materials available for distribution?

Are there informative publications and materials available for distribution?

Has a follow-up welcoming plan been developed?

Epilogue

Two ordinary men traveled the Emmaus Road. As they talked about the incredible events that occurred on Good Friday, a Stranger suddenly joined them.

The third Man asked questions about recent events in their city. The travelers were shocked that He seemed unaware of the public crucifixion of one named Jesus. They poured out their bewilderment and anxiety. He listened—and then spoke. Beginning with the story of Moses, he led them through the Scriptures on an incredible journey.

The Stranger's words overwhelmed the two men. When it appeared He would leave them, they urged Him to stay with them for supper. He did, and there, Jesus revealed himself to them. What a revelation! The grave was finally conquered!

Suddenly, He was gone. On reflection, the two travelers said, "Did not our heart burn within us while He talked with us on the road, and while He opened the Scriptures to us?" (Luke 24:32, NKJV).

Two thousand years later, the celebration that began on the Emmaus Road continues. Jesus still lives and reigns. The Scriptures are yet alive with words of hope and truth. Hearts still burn when His Word comes alive.

Two thousand years later, children, teens, and adults gather together weekly in a network of small groups called Sunday School or Bible study. They are led by teachers whose burning hearts are aflame with a passion for taking care of people and teaching the words of life.

Two thousand years later, the words of life burned in the heart of Cora Gascon. At a recent Louisiana District Sunday School Convention, she celebrated the memory of the time W. T. and Helen Johnson visited her and invited her to Sunday School in Vivian, Louisiana. There were many visits after that first one. Cora, now in her 80s and vitally alert, recalled the zealous, burning hearts of the Johnsons. She said, "They found me on a French bayou, a Frenchwoman living 25 hours a day for the devil. They just kept coming after me. They got me in Sunday School. I got saved a few weeks later, and I've been a happy, happy Christian ever since."

Many things have changed in the almost 60 years since W. T. and Helen Johnson invited Cora to Sunday School. One thing has not changed. Christ lives, and He loves through hearts and lives that have walked and talked with the Man who conquered the grave, and who said, "I am the resurrection and the life. He who believes in Me, though he may die, he shall live" (John 11:25, NKJV).

Notes

Preface

1. Roy Zuck, *The Holy Spirit in Your Teaching* (Cincinnati: Scripture Press, 1963), 11.

Chapter 1

1. Thom Rainer, *Giant Awakenings* (Nashville: Broadman and Holman, 1995), 53.

2. Mark Vainikka quoted in Elmer L. Towns, *Evangelism and Church Growth* (Ventura, Calif.: Regal Books, 1995), 226.

Chapter 2

1. Phil Roberts, *On Mission* (May-June 1999).

Chapter 3

1. Ken Hemphill, *Revitalizing the Sunday Morning Dinosaur* (Nashville: Broadman and Holman, 1996), 27-30.

2. *USA Today* quoted in *On Mission* (May-June 1999): 25.

3. Stan Toler, *ABCs of Evangelism* (Atlanta: INJOY, 1995), 24.

4. Michael Green, *Evangelism in the Early Church* (Grand Rapids: Eerdmans, 1971), 72.

5. Dale Galloway, *Strategies for Today's Leader*, vol. 6, No. 2 (spring 1999): 4.

Chapter 4

1. Christian A. Schwarz, *Natural Church Development: A Guide to Eight Essential Qualities of Healthy Churches* (Carol Stream, Ill.: ChurchSmart Resources, 1998), 29.

2. Peter Wagner, *The Healthy Church* (Ventura, Calif.: Regal Books, 1996), 17.

3. Albert M. Wells Jr., *Inspiring Quotations* (Nashville: Thomas Nelson Publishing Co., 1988), 196.

4. Peter Wagner, "Prayerlessness = powerlessness," *Good News* (May-June 1999): 10.

5. Stan Toler, *Minute Motivators* (Kansas City: Beacon Hill Press of Kansas City, 1996), 48.

Chapter 5

1. Lyle E. Schaller, "Busting Common Myths About Expansion and Change," *Leadership* (winter 1997): 48.

2. Jack Hayford, "How Many Did You Have Last Sunday?" *Christianity Today* (winter 1998): 39.

3. Wagner, *Healthy Church*, 16.

4. Gary McIntosh, *Church Growth Network Newsletter*, vol. 7, No. 2 (March 1999): 4.

5. George W. Bullard, *Net Results*, vol. 19, No. 10 (October 1998): 26.

Chapter 6

1. Stan Toler, *The People Principle: Transforming Laypersons into Leaders* (Kansas City: Beacon Hill Press of Kansas City, 1997), 101-2.

2. Herb Miller, "Reinventing the Sunday School in Childless Churches," *Net Results,* vol. 17, No. 3 (March 1996): 11.

Chapter 7

1. Randal Denny, "Sunday School Is More Important than We Think," *Preacher's Magazine* (June, July, August 1999): 17.

2. Josh Hunt, *You Can Double Your Class in Two Years or Less* (Loveland, Colo.: Group Publishing, Inc., 1997), 111.

Chapter 8

1. Stan Toler, *God Has Never Failed Me, but He Sure Has Scared Me to Death a Few Times* (Tulsa, Okla.: Honor Books, 1995), 103.

2. Stan Toler, *How to Go to Multiple Sunday Schools* video (Elkton, Md.: Church Growth Institute).